ACPL ITEM
DISCARDED

6ᴽ
Neaga, Gregor.
Fire in the computer room,
what now?

S0-ECM-901

What Now?

Disaster Recovery:
Preparing for Business Survival

Gregor Neaga

Bruce Winters

Pat Laufman

To join a Prentice Hall PTR internet mailing list,
point to http://www.prenhall.com/mail_lists/

Prentice Hall PTR
Upper Saddle River, New Jersey 07458
www.prenhall.com

Library of Congress Cataloging in Publication Data

Neaga, Gregor.
 Fire in the computer room, what now?: disaster recovery, preparing for busi-
ness survival / Gregor Neaga, Bruce Winters, Pat Laufman.
     p.   cm.
 Includes bibliographical references and index.
 ISBN 0-13-754391-3 (alk. paper)
     1. Data recovery (Computer science) 2. Business—Data processing—Secu-
rity measures—Planning. I. Winters, Bruce II. Laufman, Pat. III. Title.
QA76.9.D348N4 1997   97-8842
658.4'77--dc21   CIP

Editorial/production supervision: *Kathleen M. Caren*
Cover design director: *Jayne Conte*
Cover design: *Kiwi Design*
Manufacturing manager: *Alexis Heydt*
Marketing manager: *Stephen Solomon*
Acquisitions editor: *Michael E. Meehan*
Editorial Assistant: *Tara Ruggiero*

Allen County Public Library
900 Webster Street
PO Box 2270
Fort Wayne, IN 46801-2270

© 1997 by International Buiness Machines
       Published by Prentice Hall PTR
       Prentice-Hall, Inc.
       A Simon & Schuster Company
       Englewood Cliffs, New Jersey 07632

Take Note!
Before using this information and the product it supports, be sure to read the general information
in Appendix C, "Special Notices" on page 189.

Comments may be addressed to: IBM Corporation, International Technical Support Organization
Dept. HYJ Mail Station P099, 522 South Road, Poughkeepsie, New York 12601-5400
Prentice Hall books are widely used by corporations and government agencies for training,
marketing, and resale.
The publisher offers discounts on this book when ordered in bulk quantities.
For more information, contact Corporate Sales Department, Phone: 800-382-3419;
FAX: 201-236-7141; E-mail: corpsales@prenhall.com
Prentice Hall PTR, One Lake Street, Upper Saddle River, NJ 07458.

All rights reserved. No part of this book may be reproduced, in any form or by any means, without
permission in writing from the publisher.

All product names mentioned herein are the trademarks of their respective owners.

Printed in the United States of America
10 9 8 7 6 5 4 3 2

ISBN 0-13-754391-3

Prentice-Hall International (UK) Limited, *London*
Prentice-Hall of Australia Pty. Limited, *Sydney*
Prentice-Hall Canada Inc., *Toronto*
Prentice-Hall Hispanoamericana, S.A., *Mexico*
Prentice-Hall of India Private Limited, *New Delhi*
Prentice-Hall of Japan, Inc., *Tokyo*
Simon & Schuster Asia Pte. Ltd., *Singapore*

Contents

Preface

Are you a computer professional who is responsible for the integrity and availability of the computer network in your organization? Do you worry whether your enterprise can survive a catastrophic failure such as fire or sabotage in its data processing equipment? If you are involved in the design, planning, or implementation of a disaster recovery solution for your organization, this book is for you.

It gives an overview of how to prepare your data processing environment so it can be recovered in the event of a disaster. It identifies and explains the processes and complexities involved, and describes the following:

- How to determine the requirements of your business processes by performing a risk analysis and a business impact analysis

- How to design and implement a recovery solution by using an alternate site, and how to provide recovery procedures to restore your data and processing services

- How to maintain and test your recovery solution

The topics discussed range from basic concepts of disaster recovery to the major technical and procedural factors you must consider when designing an effective disaster recovery solution.

This book guides you through a complete *cycle* of analysis, design, and implementation of disaster recovery. While a short book like this cannot supply all the technical expertise needed to actually perform all required design and implementation work, it will help you manage the complexities of the subject. You may need a team of consultants and technical experts, like IBM's Business Recovery Services, to do the work, but this book will help you ask the right questions to get a complete job done.

Many of the considerations pertaining to disaster recovery are independent of any particular computer brand or architecture, and for the most part, no specific products are discussed.

However, we believe the IBM S/390 offers the richest platform for a disaster solution in terms of recoverability, availability, recovery data management, and workload management. An appendix illustrates some of these concepts by showing how they are implemented in hardware and software components within the S/390 platform.

How This Book Is Organized

The book is organized as follows:

- "Introduction"

    This section provides an overview of on-site recovery versus disaster recovery to highlight the importance of implementing a disaster recovery solution for the DP resources of an enterprise. The introduction discusses types of disasters, as well as the responsibilities of senior level management in determining the recovery solution.

    This section also introduces a six-step structured approach to plan, design, and implement a disaster recovery solution that meets your business needs. These six steps are discussed in detail in the six subsequent chapters.

- "Determine What the Business Requires"

    This chapter discusses *risk analysis* and *business impact analysis*. It explains the ingredients of these two processes and how they are used to assess the risk to businesses of various types of disasters, as well as the impact of an outage on each business process.

- "Determine the Data Processing Requirements"

    This chapter covers the conversion of the business requirements into data processing terms. This is where the system designer determines such things as the required recovery time, maximum allowable data loss, processor resources required to run, gigabytes of disk storage required, and dependencies on other applications or data.

This chapter also discusses service level agreements and examines the need for cooperation between organizational or departmental boundaries to reach consensus on the recovery solution.

- "Design the Backup/Recovery Solution"

  This chapter shows how to define the overall characteristics and major elements of the solution. These elements describe, in a generic way, any special hardware and software functions required for the backup and recovery processes, the recovery location, and the recovery configuration as well as network and interconnection structures.

- "Select Products to Match the Design"

  This chapter discusses how to select a specific alternate site, and hardware and software products to match the recovery solution design. It also covers how the cost of the solution can be assessed once you select the products.

- "Implement the Backup/Recovery Solution"

  This chapter covers the steps and issues related to the building or contracting of an alternate site and the development of the disaster recovery plan.

  It also describes the development of the procedures needed to facilitate regular data backup as well as the recovery process in the event of a disaster.

- "Keep the Solution Up-to-Date"

  This chapter describes the processes required to keep the recovery solution viable. The processes covered in this chapter include maintenance, auditing, and testing of the disaster recovery plan.

- Appendix A, "System/390 Disaster Recovery Products"

This section describes a number of hardware and software products and features available in the System/390 platform that can contribute to an effective disaster recovery solution.

- Appendix B, "Disaster Recovery Tiers - SHARE 78 Definition"

  In 1992, during their 78th semi-annual conference, the association of IBM customers with large computing systems (SHARE) outlined seven examples (tiers) of increasingly sophisticated disaster recovery approaches. They are included here for reference and discussion.

Comments Welcome

Your comments are important to us!

We want our redbooks to be as helpful as possible. Please send us your comments about this or other redbooks in one of the following ways:

- Fax the evaluation form found in -- Heading 'EVAL' unknown -- to the fax number shown on the form.
- Use the electronic evaluation form found on the Redbooks Home Pages at the following URLs:

  For Internet users   `http://www.redbooks.ibm.com`
  For IBM Intranet users   `http://w3.itso.ibm.com/redbooks`

- Send us a note at the following address:

  `redbook@vnet.ibm.com`

The Team That Wrote This Book

This book was produced by a team of specialists from around the world working at the International Technical Support Organization, Poughkeepsie Center.

Gregor Neaga is a Systems Management, Continuous Availability, and Disaster Recovery Specialist at the International Technical Support Organization, Poughkeepsie Center. He has been with IBM for 27 years in various positions and foreign assignments. He has worked as a systems programmer, systems engineer, storage management expert, and, for the last eight years, as a systems design consultant. Before joining the ITSO in 1996, he worked as a senior consultant at IBM UBG, the Enterprise Consulting subsidiary of IBM Germany.

Pat Laufman is a Consultant in Business Recovery Services in Canada. She has 10 years of experience in the Disaster Recovery field and over 20 years of experience in large systems. Her areas of expertise include the planning and implementation of mid-range and large system recovery plans for business and technology. She has written several articles on the different aspects of Disaster Recovery and has given presentations at various Disaster Recovery conferences.

Bruce Winters is a Technical Specialist in Business Recovery Services in Australia. He has 7 years of experience in the Disaster Recovery field and has worked at IBM and ISSC for 17 years. His areas of expertise include the design, evaluation, and implementation of disaster recovery solutions to meet business requirements. He has written extensively on disaster recovery and has contributed to all four Disaster Recovery Library publications.

Contributors to earlier editions of this book are:

John Crooks   IBM Australia

Robert Telli   IBM Switzerland
Glenda Wheeler   IBM South Africa

We would also like to thank the people who reviewed the
document, corrected errors, and suggested changes and
additions:

Pierluigi Buratti   IBM Italy
Stefan Burgmann   IBM Germany
Gaetano Cighetti   IBM Italy
Peter J. Clarke   IBM UK
David Petersen   IBM S/390 Parallel Center, USA

Further thanks to the staff and the editorial team of the
International Technical Support Organization, Poughkeepsie.

Introduction

The drive to the office is slow. The traffic is much heavier than usual for a weekday morning in July. You crane your neck in an attempt to see around the vehicles in front for the cause of the tie-up. In the distance you can hear sirens and see flashing lights; it must be a bad accident or something. When you roll down the window to get some air, the smell of acrid smoke drifts in and you realize that the holdup is not caused by a traffic accident but by a *fire*. The smoke is visible now in the skyline ahead.

Your mind starts to race as you realize that the blaze is in the vicinity of the office complex at 26 Bankers Avenue, where you manage the second floor data center of a large financial institution. Suddenly the radio announcer cuts into the music program you were listening to with a news bulletin: an early morning fire has destroyed the first three floors of 26 Bankers

Avenue! As you sit there stunned, your cellular phone begins to ring. The phone was supplied by your company for emergency use, and only the CEO and corporate executives have the number. It's the CEO calling now, and he wants to know what you're going to do to salvage the company's electronic records. You *have* planned for this...haven't you?

The scenario we just described is a *disaster.* It represents a very different situation from the routine outages that sometimes occur in computing environments.

Operations staff members are familiar with most problems that cause minor outages and in many cases can deal with them quickly and efficiently, right on site. For example, if a disk drive fails, they (hopefully) have backup tapes as well as spare disk space, and the data can be restored on an alternate device within a short time. Any failure of a hardware component for which a spare is available may bring the system down, but such an outage situation is not considered "disastrous"; even if systems are down for a day, most businesses can get by.

But imagine a situation that brings your computer operations down for a week or a month; imagine losing all company disk data, all on-site backup tapes, and the destruction of the system processor. How would you handle such a catastrophe? If, faced with this situation, you have to ask the question "What now?" it's already too late! The only effective way to cope with disasters is to have a comprehensive, fully tested disaster recovery solution in place *before* it is needed. This book will help you plan, design, and implement a disaster recovery solution to meet your business needs.

Essentially then, a disaster can be described as a problem that cannot be resolved on site within an acceptable period of time, and that requires the use of an alternate computing facility. Obvious examples are major fires, explosions, evacuations, and so on.

Sometimes, however, a minor component problem that appears to be recoverable through normal problem management procedures can also escalate into a disaster.

Suppose you had data corruption on a disk. You recover the data from a backup tape. Then you start having data errors on multiple volumes on various strings. If neither your nor the vendors' support experts can identify the source of the problem or find a fix, and the problem escalates throughout the day, management may be forced to declare a disaster and recover at an alternate facility. This is also considered to be a disaster situation.

In the context of this book, a *disaster* is defined as an extended service interruption of the data processing (DP) services of an organization which cannot be corrected within an acceptable predetermined time frame, and which necessitates the use of an alternate site or alternate equipment for recovery.

Management must determine the time frame that moves an outage from "problem" status to "disaster" status. Most organizations will accomplish this by performing a *business impact analysis* to determine the maximum allowable downtime for critical business functions.

Why do You Need Disaster Recovery?

As organizations have become more and more dependent on data processing (DP) to conduct their business and to stay competitive, the availability of the processing facilities has become crucial. Today, most businesses require a high, if not continuous, level of DP availability.

As a consequence, most businesses would find it extremely difficult to function without data processing. Manual procedures, if they exist at all, would only be practical for a short period of time. A lengthy outage in a computing environment can result in significant financial losses, especially if management liability is involved. More importantly, one can lose customer credibility and subsequent market share. In some cases, such losses could lead to the total failure of the business.

The question can be asked, "Why do I need a disaster recovery plan if I am insured?" The answer is that while business insurance may cover the material costs of an organization's assets in the event of a disaster, it will *not* recover the business. It will not keep customers, and in most cases, it will not provide up-front funds to keep the business going until it is recovered.

A study performed by the University of Minnesota has shown that more than 60% of businesses that suffer a disaster and do not have a working Disaster Recovery Plan will go out of business within 2 to 3 years. With increased dependency on DP availability, this number will probably go up.

Therefore, the ability to successfully recover from a disaster within a predetermined time frame should be a crucial element of an organization's strategic business plan.

Types of Disasters

Although it is impossible to come up with a complete list of all types of disasters, several categories can be identified:

Local site disasters are events that are limited to a specific area, room, or location of a building (for example, the computer room). This type of disaster can be the result of:

- Fire
- Flooding
- Catastrophic machine failure
- Sabotage
- Power failure

Site disasters affect the whole building and can be caused by such events as:

- Bombings
- Explosions
- Fire
- Flood
- Power outages

Area disasters generally affect the vicinity or area where the building is located. This area may cover a radius of several miles and can be caused by:

- Bombings
- Earthquakes
- Environmental contamination
- Explosions
- Outbreaks of disease

- Plane crashes
- Volcanic eruptions
- Wind or snow storms
- Terrorist attacks

In some of the above situations, the DP equipment may still be intact and usable, but is simply inaccessible. With preplanning, you may be able to run the data center from a remote location for a short period of time.

Recent statistics on the most common types of disasters that occur internationally show that terrorism and fire are the most common causes of disasters (see Figure 1).

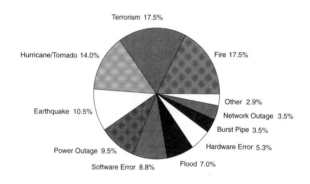

Figure 1. *Worldwide Disaster Frequency by Type.*
Source: Contingency Planning Research Inc. This data is based on 57 disaster incidents since 1988.

Disaster Avoidance

It stands to reason that the more preventive measures that are put in place, the less chance there is of a situation resulting in a disaster to the organization. However, no matter how sophisticated these preventive measures are, there will always be some risk of an outage. You can reduce the risk of disasters as you increase the cost of preventing them.

Certain measures should be taken to help prevent disasters from affecting your organization or to minimize their impact when they are unavoidable. The best way to determine which measures your organization should include is to conduct a *risk analysis* to determine where the organization's major vulnerabilities are.

The minimum preventive measures are usually good on-site recovery procedures to help avoid having routine problems escalate into a disaster. This requires, for instance, spare hardware, regular backups, and a skilled operations staff. In addition, you may have to consider things like building fortification, improved fire protection, rigorous access control and other operational procedures and corporate policies. The time and cost involved in implementing and maintaining such measures can be justified through comparison with the time and cost involved in dealing with the situation at the time of a disaster.

If, in spite of the preventive measures, a potentially disastrous incident occurs, you will have to determine if it requires *on site* recovery or *disaster* recovery procedures, as shown in Figure 2. The situation is not necessarily obvious, so the decision criteria have to be carefully prepared as part of planning and implementing a disaster recovery solution.

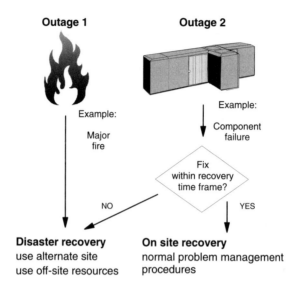

Figure 2. *On-Site Recovery versus Disaster Recovery*

Plan and Implement a Disaster Recovery Solution

This book suggests a structured approach to planning and implementing a disaster recovery solution to meet your company's business requirements. Here, we will introduce and summarize the six steps in this structured approach. Subsequent chapters of the book will depict each step of this approach.

Designing and implementing a suitable disaster recovery solution is not a simple task. It can involve considerable effort and expense, especially if you are starting from scratch. A solution involves the following activities:

- It must be designed and built to match the business requirements.

- It may require the building or modification of a data processing site.

- It will certainly require the development and testing of many new procedures, and these new procedures and processes must be compatible with existing operations. Staff from many different departments will be involved, and they must work together when developing and implementing the solution.

- It will involve a trade-off between cost, recovery speed, completeness of recovery, and the scope of disasters covered.

As with any design project, a structured approach helps to ensure that all of these factors are considered and suitably addressed.

Figure 3 on page 12 shows the main activities required in the planning and implementing of a disaster recovery capability. These activities are:

1. Determining what the business requires

   During this initial part of the process, a *risk analysis* and a *business impact analysis* should be conducted to determine what the business requirements are. Many business processes are so dependent upon DP that they cannot be performed any more in the event of a disaster. These processes must be evaluated for their negative impact, that is, loss of business and revenue. There might be regulatory reasons, too, that require a business process to be available at all times. This analysis will tell you what your business process priorities are and what recovery time scale is required for each business process. Also, a disaster bears the risk that the organization loses track of some business transactions that were in process when the disaster occurred. The business impact analysis will have to determine to what degree such a loss can be tolerated for each business process. The results can be used in the next step to determine the DP requirements.

2. Determining the data processing requirements

Once the business requirements have been established, you must convert them into data processing terms, or into a context that the system designer can use. The result should be a matrix showing, for each application, the required recovery time, maximum allowable data loss, computing power required to run, disk storage required, and dependencies on other applications or data. A good deal of cooperation across organizational and departmental boundaries will be necessary to reach a consensus on requirements with which everyone is happy.

3. Designing the backup/recovery solution

After the DP requirements have been established and agreed upon, you must develop and design the backup and recovery solution. In this context, design means to define the overall characteristics and major elements of the solution. These elements describe, in a generic way, any special hardware and software functions required for the backup and recovery processes, the recovery location, the recovery configuration as well as network and interconnection structures. Often, a high level design is sufficient in order to estimate the cost of the solution. If the cost is too high, the solution will need to be reworked until both the cost and the solution are agreed upon. Once the

3 1833 03233 9019

solution decision is definite, a more detailed design is required.

4. Selecting products to match the design

Having built the design for the recovery solution, you are ready to select the products required to implement that solution. Some consideration of products was probably done during the initial design phase, but now you must select products that can be used together to support the recovery design solution you developed. This selection again influences the cost of the solution.

"Products" will consist of hardware, software, and possibly the selection of an alternate site.

5. Implementing the backup/recovery solution

You are now ready to implement the recovery solution according to the design that was developed. To do this, you must make arrangements regarding the alternate site, install any required hardware and software components, and develop the disaster recovery plan.

The development of the recovery plan requires a project on its own. You must set up the recovery teams, develop and implement backup and recovery procedures, and document the recovery steps to execute the recovery at the time of a disaster.

6. Keeping the solution up-to-date

Implementing the disaster recovery solution can be a long and involved process, but you must also put procedures in place to ensure that the recovery solution remains viable regardless of changes at the primary or alternate site. Do this by developing and implementing procedures for the maintenance, testing, and auditing of the recovery plan.

The following figure illustrates this structured approach to disaster recovery.

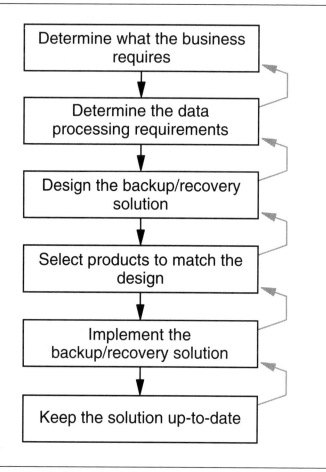

Figure 3. *A Structured Approach to Disaster Recovery*

Iterative Design

Often, the activities we just described do not follow each other strictly in sequence.

In some instances, implementation work may start even while portions of the solution design are still being developed.

In other instances, the activities associated with a certain step are achieved in an earlier step. For example, an organization may decide to use a specific second site even before the full business requirements are established.

More importantly, you will often reach a point in the design process where some aspect of the solution causes you to rework an earlier stage. In this case, the process flow may have to *loop back* and modify the requirements or the design.

A very common requirement is to estimate the costs of various options. Typically, a high-level pass is taken through the requirements, design, and product selection steps to estimate the cost of various options. This allows certain options to be ignored and the more plausible options to be reworked.

You might not agree with the proposed sequence altogether. For instance, some people might submit that, in many cases, you have to look at available products (step 4) before you can come up with the overall design (step 3). We'd like to leave these arguments to the experts (for instance, disaster recovery consultants) who do the design in each individual case. Rather than debating this, we'd like to say at this point that this book is less an exercise in system design theory than a comprehensive discussion of planning topics pertaining to disaster recovery.

Make Trade-offs in Disaster Recovery

Although you want to develop a disaster recovery solution that exactly matches the requirements of your business, you must be aware that some requirements are trade-offs, or are even mutually exclusive. In addition, the more stringent the requirements, the higher the cost of the solution.

These are the four main factors that need to be traded off in any solution:

1. How fast must the recovery be accomplished?
2. How much data can be lost?
3. What type of disaster does the solution cover?
4. What is the cost of the solution?

Figure 4 on page 15 shows the relationship between these factors.

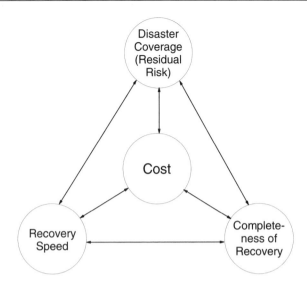

Figure 4. *Decision Criteria for an Individual Disaster Recovery Design*

Throughout the planning and design process, you need to be aware of these factors and balance them to develop a solution which best meets the business needs at an acceptable cost. This trade-off triangle is discussed in more detail later in the book as it applies to the various steps.

Recovery Management and Project Ownership

Despite the many technical aspects involved, disaster recovery planning, or business continuity planning in general, is a corporate issue, and not primarily a data processing issue. After all, the only reason the data center is recovered is to allow the organization's business functions and services to continue. Therefore, deciding on an appropriate disaster recovery strategy may require:

• Major investments and appropriate cost justification

Obvious examples are the costs associated with contracting to an alternate hot site facility or, if necessary, the costs for the construction of a new building (including the installation of high bandwidth interconnection facilities, and spare processor and disk resources). Investments of such magnitude must be appropriately cost-justified.

- Analyzing the importance and priority of business processes

  The amount of effort and cost that goes into the design and implementation of a disaster recovery strategy often cannot be justified for all DP applications. Therefore, a detailed analysis of the relative importance and priority of DP related business processes is required.

- Major changes in the data processing "culture"

  A particular disaster recovery strategy may create the need to impose new rules on application development, systems operation, and user departments.

- Conscious acceptance of residual risks

  Whatever disaster recovery strategy is taken, there will never be complete coverage against all possible disasters. In most cases, the adopted strategy is a compromise derived from such opposing factors as recovery completeness, speed, and cost. The residual risk that remains should be understood and consciously accepted. It must also be re-evaluated periodically as business goals and processes evolve.

- Senior management commitment to the ongoing support of the recovery strategy

Therefore, although disaster recovery planning is likely to be executed by DP professionals, it should be owned and driven by high-level business management.

Determine What the Business Requires

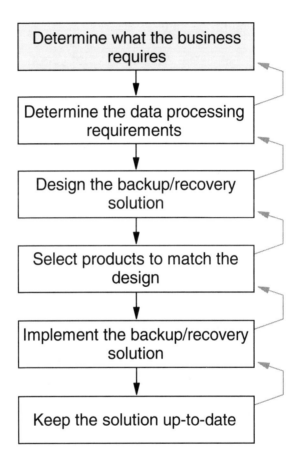

The first step in developing a disaster recovery solution for the DP resources is to determine exactly what is needed by the business. To achieve this, a *risk analysis* and a *business impact analysis* should be conducted to determine what the business requirements are. Many business processes are so dependent upon DP that they cannot be performed any more in the event of a disaster. These processes must be evaluated for their negative impact, that is, loss of business and revenue. There might be regulatory reasons, too, that require a business process to be available at all times.

This analysis will tell you what your business process priorities are and what recovery time scale is required for each business process. Also, a disaster bears the risk that the organization loses track of some business transactions that were in process when the disaster occurred. The business impact analysis will have to determine to what degree such a loss can be tolerated for each business process. The results can be used in the next step to determine the DP requirements. We will discuss these DP requirements in the subsequent chapter.

Why Analyze the Requirements?

You must analyze your business requirements to determine what your disaster recovery strategy will be.

There are two main areas to consider when determining requirements:

- To what type of risk is the organization vulnerable?

  Not all organizations face the same risks to the same degree. For instance, some buildings are endangered by fire more than others. Some areas are susceptible to earthquakes, others to floods. A *risk analysis* can help determine this exposure.

- How long an outage can your critical business functions sustain?

  A utility billing system, like the one that prints your monthly electricity or telephone bill, may be able to sustain an outage of several days without jeopardizing current and future business. For a banking, stock market, or mail order entry system an outage of a few hours can be fatal.

A *business impact analysis* will help you determine the length of time you can afford to be without your system working.

Together, the results of these two analyses will show you what business requirements the recovery solution must address.

There is a temptation to classify *all* business processes as highly important and to demand the best possible recovery capabilities for all of them. When defining your recovery resource requirements, remember that the investment needed to provide a viable disaster recovery solution can be substantial. Whether the solution involves disaster recovery at another company site or is accomplished through a contractual agreement with a third party vendor, the cost of hardware, software, and possible building construction can be very high. For this reason, it is prudent to limit resource requirements only to those that are *critical* and *essential* to the survival of the business.

A risk analysis should result in the following:

- A determination of what preventative measures are required
- A determination of what type of disaster recovery is required
- A conscious acceptance of the risks not covered by the first two measures

Implementing preventative measures reduces the risk of disaster and may minimize the impact if a disaster should occur, while implementing a disaster recovery strategy provides protection against risks not covered by preventative measures.

However, in some instances, there may be risks that an organization consciously chooses not to cover in its disaster recovery strategy.

For example, a laboratory and its data center might be located in the same premises. If a disaster occurs and is limited to the data center, then the recovery plan will be invoked, and processing is restored at an alternate data center. If, however, the whole building (including the laboratory) is destroyed, no plan would be invoked. The organization has chosen not to provide an alternate building, so there would be no need for data processing without the laboratory.

You can make recovery determinations like these regarding your business by using risk analysis and business impact analysis.

Analyze the Risk of a Disaster

Performing a risk analysis exposes an organization's vulnerabilities that could result in loss of assets and critical business functions.

In order to consistently minimize the impact of a disaster, an in-depth study, as well as periodic reviews should be conducted to determine the risk of various categories of disasters occurring in the area (or in a particular type of business) and the degree to which these disasters would affect the business. This will then determine the risk of each category of disaster affecting your data processing operation.

The risk analysis should include (but not be limited to) the following areas:

- Physical security

  The issues relating to the building or facility itself, such as intrusion prevention and building specifications for fire and structure.

- Data security

  The procedures put in place to ensure the integrity of information systems data throughout the organization.

- Disgruntled employees

  Practices and procedures designed to intercept possible negative actions by disgruntled employees. Such practices may include escorting employees out of the building immediately upon dismissal.

- Backup and recovery systems

  An analysis of the backup and recovery procedures currently in place to protect the data and hardware components critical to the data processing capability of the organization.

- Vulnerability of the infrastructure

  This analysis covers issues such as redundant power supplies, uninterrupted power supply (UPS), telephone feeds, and water supplies.

- Location of data center

  Focusing on the physical location of the data center within the building as well as the location of the building itself, in order to determine disasters to which the data center may be highly susceptible, such as floods or earthquakes. If the building itself is in an area susceptible to flooding, then the data center should not be located in the basement.

- Key skills

Asks whether the organization is dependent on specific key skills or individuals and if a disaster could result in the loss of these individuals. Consideration must be given to duplicating these skills with training, education, and the implementation of comprehensive procedures and documentation.

The result of the analysis could be expressed as a table showing the likelihood of each threat and the potential outage duration that could result. With such a table, management can make a conscious decision about the scopes of failure that are to be covered and, most importantly, those that are not.

Based on the results, a high level decision might be made to protect against "local disasters" (say, within a block or two), but not against regional or national disasters.

There is no practical and affordable disaster recovery strategy that can protect against all possible threats. For instance, most organizations will implement a strategy that protects against local disasters, but few will cover national or even global disasters. Also, organizations that run two or more DP operations may have a recovery strategy that works in the event that one site gets destroyed, but not if multiple sites are destroyed at the same time.

Consequently, there will always be some residual risk to be taken. The decision about the scope of disaster to be prepared for should be made at the highest levels of the organization. The specific residual risks should be explicitly documented and consciously accepted.

Why Not Take the Risk?

While it is economically and functionally impossible to protect an organization against all conceivable risks, a comprehensive recovery plan that ensures prompt recovery from an unavoidable interruption of service is essential!

Besides the impact to the business, there are a number of other reasons you may decide that it is not worth taking the risk. These range from external pressures to internal policies.

- External Pressures

  External pressures could come from external auditors, the press, and regulatory bodies such as government agencies.
- Internal Policies

  Internal policies include such elements as internal auditors, corporate policies, and unions.

The ultimate question to be asked is, "Are you prepared to sacrifice your business to a disaster?"

Analyze the Business Processes

The other part of understanding your business requirements for disaster recovery is to determine the impact of an outage on your business processes. Before discussing the considerations to be taken in analyzing the business processes, we should make the distinction between a *business process* and an *application*.

A business process refers to a group of related activities that support the successful operation of the business or its services. An application refers to a collection of related DP jobs or online systems designed to support the business processes. For example, an airline may have a data processing application called "reservations." Within this application could be several business processes such as ticketing, air travel points, boarding, and so forth.

In some cases, a business process may require the support of more than one application.

Initially, only the most critical business processes may be recovered. But which are the critical processes? And how critical is critical? Are there services that must be recovered within hours, or can the outage extend to days? Also, although some services may tolerate longer outages, all services must be recovered eventually. So in what order should they be recovered? These questions can be answered by conducting a business impact analysis.

The analysis of the business processes should define:

- Which business processes should be included in the scope of a recovery
- The cost (dollars, lost revenue, lost customers and so on) of an outage to each business process
- The maximum allowable outage for each business process
- The recovery priority for business processes
- The dependencies between business processes
- The level of unrecoverable transactions that will be acceptable by each business unit in the event of a disaster (see note following)

Note: Obviously the aim is to recover *all* transactions as soon as possible; however, there may be instances where data cannot be recovered or recreated, or where data can be recovered but not for a significant amount of time. Whether you are able to fully recover all transactions that were entered at the time of the disaster depends on the available DP hardware and software technology, and it can be a major cost factor.

As in the case of the risk analysis, the business impact analysis may be done through a formal study in order to accurately determine the various impacts to all business functions. In many organizations, however, senior management is well aware of which business functions or processes are critical to the survival of the organization. In the case of a mid-range system that can be fully recovered within 24 hours, management will probably decide to restore the whole system rather than go to the time and trouble of performing an in-depth business impact analysis.

DP Related Business Processes

The first step in the analysis is to determine all of the business processes that are DP-related. It may be necessary to begin at the application level in order to ensure that all business processes are included in the analysis. Once the processes have been identified, the actual analysis can be conducted at the business process level. (Note that as part of a total Business Recovery Plan, all business processes should be analyzed. In this document, however, we are concerned only with those processes that are supported by DP.)

Impact of an Outage

Next, for each process, the actual business impact of an outage should be determined.

Impact criteria may include:

- Outage cost over time

  What is the impact to the organization in terms of lost revenue and profit?

- Lost business

  Lost business will almost certainly be a fact during the actual interruption, but a significant amount of business loss will occur through the future loss of market share resulting from the outage. Customers who take their business to a competitor during the outage and are happy with the service will probably not bother to change back once the disaster is over.

- Legal/regulatory ramifications

  Business contracts should be examined to see if they contain penalties for failure to comply with things such as service levels or availability. There may also be some government regulations that could place the organization in a compromising position in the event of a disaster.

The following are some mitigating factors that may reduce the impact caused by the criteria just discussed:

- If manual procedures are in place, business processes could manage without data processing for a longer period of time.
- Cross-training of personnel will increase the probability of technical or business expertise being available at time of disaster.
- Existing backup and recovery procedures

One of the most important factors that influences the recovery solution is the outage cost in relation to the outage time. In general, the cost to the business of losing a given service increases as the length of the outage increases. This is illustrated in Figure 5 on page 27.

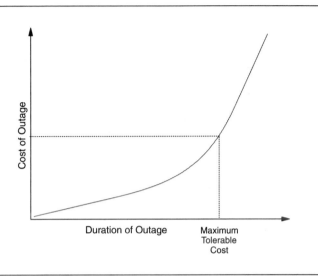

Figure 5. *Outage Cost and Outage Time*

By summing the cost curves for each business process, you can also plot the outage cost versus outage time for the business as a whole.

Maximum Acceptable Outage

The maximum acceptable service outage for each business process should now be defined. This may be based on the outage cost reaching an unacceptable level or, more simply, on an assessment of how the outage affected your business, such as a change in customer perception, lost image and so on. Either way, a maximum tolerable outage should be determined for each business process. Depending on the organization's type of business, other considerations may be involved in determining the maximum tolerable outage time. Many organizations have business contracts with suppliers, unions, and other outside agencies. Will the business be prepared to fulfill the legal requirements of these contracts in the event of a disaster?

Recovery Priority

In planning for disaster recovery, one important principle should be remembered: eventually, all of the workload must be recovered. Some services may be required immediately, others after days, and still others after weeks or months. Some data will be recovered from backups, while some will have to be recreated. But eventually, all workload must be restored. You may want to assign criticality levels to the business processes based on their maximum acceptable outages. These levels cannot, however, be defined in absolute terms, because criticality is a relative measure that is a function of time.

At least three levels of criticality can be used:

High Criticality (critical):   Business processes that are identified as being highly critical are the most important to your business. Loss of the capability to process information would result in an immediate and serious impact on the organization's ability to maintain the services it provides to its customers or users. Typically, a highly critical business process must be recovered within 24 hours.

Medium Criticality (important): Business processes in this category are those where the loss of the capability to process information would have a serious impact on the ability of the organization to effectively operate. Typically, these business processes must be recovered within 48 hours.

Low Criticality (low importance): These include business processes where the loss of the capability to process information would not have an immediate or serious impact on the ability of the organization to service the informational needs of its customers or users. Typically, these business processes can wait for many days or even weeks for recovery.

It was mentioned earlier that criticality is a function of time. Therefore, there is no reason to classify business processes as *not important* or *non-critical*. Even if a process is classified as of low importance, the moment will come when the criticality level changes from low to medium and finally to high. For example, it is common to regard application development as having low priority. However, even application development will become critical after a time.

The criticality level can depend on the time when a disaster occurs. Payroll services could be of medium criticality in the middle of the month, but could be highly critical at the end of a month. The disaster recovery strategy must satisfy the worst case.

Business processes can change their level of criticality. A low criticality function, for example, could gradually become highly critical as business changes occur. The business processes should be reviewed periodically to allow for these changes.

Criticality, priority, and importance can be considered as synonyms in this discussion.

Loss of Transactions

Figure 5 on page 27 focuses on the relationship between the cost of an outage and the outage time. However, the other potential cost of an outage is the loss of data.

When a disaster occurs and the disaster recovery plan is invoked, the data will typically be restored to a level it was at sometime before the disaster. As a result, there will be data transactions that will not be recovered at this point. Some of these transaction will be recreated; however, others may not be recreated. The business impact analysis should determine whether transactions could be recreated from other sources and what level of transaction loss, if any, is acceptable for each business process.

Determine the Data Processing Requirements

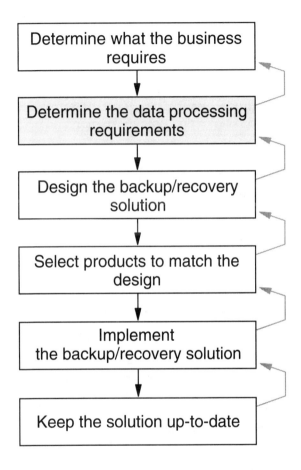

Determine what the business requires

Determine the data processing requirements

Design the backup/recovery solution

Select products to match the design

Implement the backup/recovery solution

Keep the solution up-to-date

Once the *risk analysis* and the *business impact analysis* have been completed, you should have all the information needed to determine the recovery requirements for the organization's critical business functions. This information must now be converted from a business context to a data processing context, in order to determine which procedures and resources are needed to support the recovery and ongoing processing at the recovery site.

There are two types of DP processes that need to be considered:

- The applications that actually make up the business processes
- The DP systems management infrastructure processes that are required to run and support the business process applications

Map the Business Requirements to the Applications

Although the purpose of disaster recovery is to restore the business processes, in practice DP recovery involves the restoration of DP applications and data. In order to design an appropriate disaster recovery solution, we must first identify the recovery requirements for the critical applications and data.

The DP department supports the business processes with its architecture, resources (hardware, software, and personnel), and operation of data processing. Once the business recovery requirements have been determined, DP management must identify the relationship between the business processes, the applications, and the data for the data processing environment.

Figure 6 on page 33 illustrates relationships between a number of business processes, the applications that support these processes, and the data accessed by these applications. In general, the recovery requirements of an application and its data are the same as the recovery requirements of the business process it supports. If a business process has a maximum tolerable outage of 12 hours, then the applications and data that support that business process must be restored and recovered in 12 hours or less. If a business process can only accept transaction loss up to an hour before the disaster, then the associated applications must be recovered in such a way as to ensure that less than one hour of data is lost.

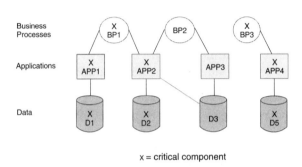

x = critical component

Figure 6. Relationship between Business Processes, Applications, and Data

Application Inventory

In order for the design of the recovery solution to be developed, the following requirements need to be determined for each application and all data:

- The maximum acceptable down time for each application (service loss)

- The maximum tolerable amount of data loss in a disaster (data loss)

- The data currency that data should have when service is resumed

   Note: Data Currency is defined as a measure of how close the restored data level matches the data level at the time of the disaster. Usually data can be restored to the level of the most recent backup, or to that of accumulated transaction logs. This level may be different from the level that existed at the time of the disaster.

- Hardware capacity requirements such as:
  - Processor capacity (processing power, storage, channels)
  - Disk capacity in gigabytes by model and types
  - Number of tape units by model and types
  - Printing requirements such as capacity, number of units, and destination
  - Other specific equipment, such as scanners and document readers

- Network requirements concerning:
  - Backup topology
  - Maximum acceptable down time
  - Transmission bandwidth
  - Which departments will be connected in disaster recovery mode

- The service levels to be maintained following the disaster

The sum of this information is often called an *application inventory*. Assessing the recovery requirements of the applications and data is typically not as simple as just assigning the requirements of each business process to its associated applications. It is complicated by a number of factors such as:

- Interdependencies of business processes and applications

A single application may support multiple business processes with different levels of criticality.

- Interdependencies of applications and data

  Some of the applications may access data on several processors, subsystems, or even different platforms, using complex connections and interfaces. Much of this data might be shared by other applications.

- Interdependencies of applications

  If a highly critical application is dependent on a less-critical one, the latter one must be classified as critical, too.

Figure 6 on page 33 depicts three business processes, two of which are deemed critical. These business processes are linked to applications, which in turn own data. Although "APP3" is not deemed critical, its data "D3" is accessed by "APP2" (a critical application) and therefore its data, "D3" must be recovered at the same time.

These complexities often result in the need to cluster multiple applications or pieces of data together and treat them essentially as a single entity.

Data may be so intertwined between many applications and online systems that any attempt to split out the data for the critical business processes only becomes impractical. In this case it may be better to recover all the data together. This would translate into more disk storage requirements at the alternate site but only enough processing power to run the applications that support the critical business processes.

Once the applications recovery requirements have been determined and the interdependencies between applications and their data have been assessed, the result is an application inventory, as illustrated in Figure 7 and Figure 8.

	Criticality Level	Outage Time	Maximum Data Loss	Data Acessed	Interrelation to Other Applications
Application 1	medium	18 hours	last 3 hours	database Pool 1	input for application n, DB2
Application 2	low	36 hours	last 500 transactions	batch pool	batch stream xyz
Application 3	high	10 minutes	none	database pool 2	none
...					
Application n	...	...	...	...	...

Figure 7. *Application Inventory List, Part 1*

	Processor Performance Units	Processor Storage (Megabytes)	Disk Storage (Gigabytes)	Network Load (Baud)	Print Volume (pages/day)
Application 1	7.0	7	1.1	2x9600	10,000
Application 2	6.1	12.8	3.6	2x64k	40,000
Application 3	1.4	6.2	0.4	1x4800	5,000
...	...	...	...	...	...
Application n	...	...	...	...	...
Total	32.0	96 MB	70 GB		160,000

Figure 8. *Application Inventory List, Part 2*

These tables document the recovery requirements of the applications: how quickly each one must be recovered, the resources that are required to recover and run the application (including disk, processor, network and printing requirements), and the interdependencies with other applications and data.

"Loss of Transactions" on page 30 discusses the potential for transactions being lost in a disaster. Transaction loss in business process translates into data loss for applications and their associated data.

The effect of data loss and the techniques to minimize it are discussed in "Orphan Data" on page 53 and "Lost Data" on page 55.

Systems Management Processes

When the application inventory has been completed, all of the DP infrastructure processes that are needed to run and support the business applications must also be identified. These are commonly referred to as systems management processes or installation management processes, and they are used to control and manage all key operational aspects of a DP installation, such as changes, problems, capacity, performance and security. These processes and their associated procedures and tools must be analyzed in order to assess which ones are required to run and support the business applications to the required service levels. All of the essential components need to be defined and passed as a requirement to the solution design phase. The basic rule is that if a component is needed to run or support a business application at the prime site, then it must be replicated at the recovery site. In practice, most (if not all) of these components are data, and therefore it is really a matter of making sure that they are backed up and restored along with all of the other critical data. See "Data Backup and Recovery Processes" on page 46.

Service Level Agreements for DR

As part of the process of analyzing the recovery requirements and deciding on a disaster recovery strategy, it is important that the users of the critical business processes are in agreement with the level of service to be delivered as a result of the selected strategy. It is recommended that this be documented in existing service level agreements, or that new agreements be created if none exists.

Service level agreements describe the scope of services, performance, and infrastructure that are to be delivered by DP. In relation to disaster recovery, service level agreements should contain statements about:

- Available applications in disaster backup processing
- Unavailable applications in disaster backup processing
- Order of application recovery
- Maximum outage duration of application
- Maximum outage duration of network connectivity
- Maximum amount of data loss
- Online and backup times of the available applications
- Expected performance and response times
- Network-connected divisions and departments, line speed, and capacity
- Print service: output delivery times, capacity, procedures
- Limitations and disclaimers
- Accounting: how departments are charged for disaster backup

Service level agreements must be reviewed periodically. Changing the disaster recovery strategy and technical solution will affect the service that will be provided.

Reach a Consensus

This chapter and the preceding chapter have described an approach to determining your requirements for a disaster recovery solution. In practice, this analysis is not always straightforward. It requires a carefully planned approach.

The functions that will be involved in the analysis of the business processes and the definition of the DP requirements will include:

- Senior management (Information Technology, Finance, and Business)
- Business process owners
- Application owners
- System support/programming
- Application support
- Systems programming
- Networking
- Operations
- Data security

Because the business needs are viewed differently by various areas of an organization, it can be difficult to arrive at a consensus of what needs to be recovered first in the event of a disaster. A project leader with a profound understanding of the business requirements should be appointed to run the analysis project, and this leader should involve the appropriate personnel and business functions as required.

If the project leader is internal to the company, there can sometimes be difficulty in crossing departmental or organizational boundaries in order to assign tasks and make decisions. Therefore, the project leader should have sufficient seniority and knowledge of the organization or sufficient support from senior management to ensure such difficulties do not arise.

It is extremely important to understand that although the functional areas will provide the detailed information extracted as part of the *business impact analysis*, it is senior management that owns the decision on what will be recovered, and when. A formal and detailed review of the results of the analysis steps should take place before the information is used as input to the next step in the process.

The following are some examples of the difficulties that may arise during the data gathering process:

- Lack of cooperation between senior executives, business units and DP management
- Lack of priority given to disaster recovery
- Underestimating or overestimating the criticality of business processes and applications
- Different valuation because of different perspectives
- Lack of understanding and education
- Missing awareness and goodwill
- Missing procedures

Make Trade-offs during Requirements Gathering

The need to balance a number of competing design factors was discussed in "Make Trade-offs in Disaster Recovery" on page 14. In theory, you should keep your business and DP requirements free of these trade-offs and cost considerations, and simply document what is required by the business. The trade-offs could then be handled in the design and costing of the solution. In practice, a great deal of effort and rework can often be saved by assessing some of these trade-offs even during the requirements gathering. For instance, a requirement for zero data loss and 1 hour recovery at a site 1000 km from the primary site is typically either technically impossible or extremely expensive.

When these types of requirements emerge as a result of the business and applications analyses, you may want either to rework the requirements with more realistic ground rules, or perform a preliminary cost estimate for the required solution to ensure that this cost is in the acceptable range for the business.

Design the Backup/Recovery Solution

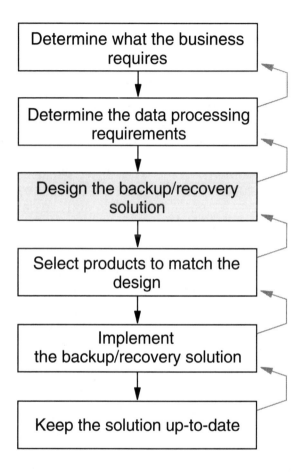

Once the data processing requirements are agreed upon, you are in a position to develop a picture or a design of the final solution, just as an architect drafts an outline or builds a cardboard model of a building.

The disaster recovery design describes, in broad terms, the overall characteristics and major elements of the target solution. These elements are listed here and discussed in the following sections:

- Scope of the recovery
- Strategy for testing
- Data backup and recovery processes
- Managing and operating the alternate site
- Description of the recovery configuration

The amount of detail in the design will depend on your purpose. If your aim at this point is to estimate the cost of one or more potential solutions, you may not require this level of detail. If, on the other hand, you have decided on a solution and are developing a final design ready for implementation, far more detail will be required.

The more detailed design depends to a large degree on appropriate functions that are available in hardware and software products. For the purpose of this book we have separated the logical design (covered in this chapter) from the product selection (covered in "Select Products to Match the Design" on page 103).

Scope of the Recovery

The disaster recovery design should clearly define the scope of the recovery, that is, what is being recovered and within what time frame. This is to ensure from the beginning that there is no confusion about what is and is not part of this recovery design. The definition of the scope should include:

- Assumptions of what types of disaster are included and excluded

- The sequence in which applications will be recovered
- The maximum recovery timing for each application
- The data that will be recovered
- The data currency of the data once it is recovered

This information will be based on the analysis of the business and application requirements (see "Determine What the Business Requires" on page 17 and "Determine the Data Processing Requirements" on page 31).

Strategy for Testing

In the design we are building there is no need to develop a detailed disaster recovery test plan. This will come later as we implement the solution we have chosen (see "Test the Plan" on page 150). However, it is useful at this stage to determine, at a high level, how testing will take place, as this may influence the complexity and the cost of our proposed solution.

Where will the testing take place? What resources will be required? Can the production network be tested? Do other workloads or data need to be removed during the test?

It may seem that testing is easier when the recovery site is a company-owned second site. Both sites are owned and managed by the company and hence planning and coordination are easier. In practice it is often difficult to test in this environment due to the need to shut down any workload already running on the recovery processor and possibly back up the data. In cases where the recovery processor normally runs a portion of the critical workload this is especially true, but it is even difficult to find appropriate times to bring down less critical workloads. Even when this is possible the test time is often extended by the need to back up the data on the disk and to restore it after the test.

Testing in your own second site often results in tests being run less frequently or less fully than would be ideal.

When there are sufficient spare resources at the recovery site or when the workload can easily and quickly be displaced, this problem is removed. In this case, in-house testing is typically very effective.

When a commercial hot site is used for recovery testing, the test needs to be scheduled with the service provider. Contention with other clients may mean that testing has to be scheduled well in advance. On the other hand, once the test window is secured, the testing should be very efficient as all the resources are ready and available to you from start to finish.

Data Backup and Recovery Processes

Before the required recovery configuration can be defined it is necessary to determine the processes for backing up and recovering the critical data. The methods used to back up the data, the way it is transported and stored off-site, and the techniques for recovering the data all influence the physical resources required at the alternate site and the interconnection between the sites.

The following discussion describes the major components of data backup and recovery processes and highlights some of the factors that need to be considered.

Of all DP resources, data is probably the most important. Other resources, such as hardware, vendor software, and building facilities are all ultimately replaceable--most data is not. Data is also the most volatile and complex of all DP resources and the most critical to the business.

This complexity and volatility of data makes it the most difficult resource to manage during recovery. Whereas the relatively static nature of hardware and building facilities enables sites to be ready before recovery is necessary, the volatile nature of data means it must be managed as an ongoing process. Either data is kept current at a recovery site or it must be made current as part of the recovery process.

Therefore, one of the key components of the disaster recovery design is the data backup and recovery strategy, that is, what data will be backed up, how often, in what way, how will it be recovered, and in what order. Although the procedures for backup and recovery are logically separate pieces of the design, they can not be designed separately because they are so closely linked. The method of backup will often determine the recovery method, but from a design point of view, the opposite approach is preferable. The recovery requirements should determine how the data will be recovered and subsequently how the backup will be performed.

The following section discusses the factors that will influence the decisions on backup and recovery techniques and timing.

Data Categories

When discussing techniques for the backup and recovery of data, it is useful to group the data into categories based on its usage and volatility. There are at least three general categories of data associated with a computer system: application data, infrastructure data, and system data. It is necessary to understand the nature of the data in each of these categories to build an effective disaster recovery plan. The data categories are described briefly below and illustrated in Figure 9 on page 50. A more detailed discussion of these categories is found in *Disaster Recovery Library Data Recovery* (see "International Technical Support Organization Publications" on page 193).

Note: In the context of backup and recovery, programs are simply a form of data that has to be addressed. The following discussion therefore covers both data and software.

Application Data

This includes all data belonging to applications (databases, work files, programs, and so on) that must be present for the applications to run. In a disaster, all this data needs to be recovered or recreated to enable application recovery.

The vital core of the application data is the business data. This is the data that pertains to the business that the computer system supports. It is the customer information, the inventory data, the customer orders or the account balances. It is either input to the computer processing or the output from the processing. It is the reason for information processing.

The primary focus in this section will be on business data; it is the most volatile, the most valuable, and the most challenging to recreate. Whereas traditional change management processes cover changes to application programs and system software, business data is usually outside the scope of systems management.

Infrastructure Data

This category, sometimes called metadata, includes subsystem data supporting the applications, such as the Database Management Systems, catalogs, and data from access control and security systems. Typically this data is subject to frequent change.

This type of data is often seen as system data; however, it is typically more volatile than system data and is more closely related to the application data. It is useful in terms of backup and recovery to treat it separately.

System Data

This includes the system platform and related files needed to IPL or "boot" an operational system. It consists of the system software tailored to a specific machine configuration. This data is typically subject to little change between new system releases. It is the most readily recreated type of data.

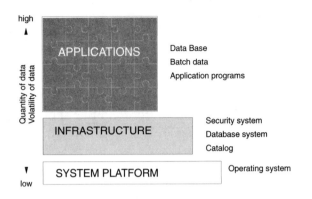

Figure 9. Data Categories

Disaster Recovery Scenario

In order to understand some of the main aspects of data backup and recovery, we need to take a look at the sequence of events and the activities required in the event of a disaster.

Figure 10 on page 51 shows the events just prior to a disaster and following a disaster. The first event shown in the sequence is a data backup. This happened at some point in time before the failure. This backup represents the data that we will recover.

Note: This may not be the last data backup taken before the failure. However, it is the last backup that was safely removed from the site before the failure.

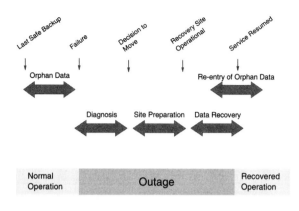

Figure 10. Disaster Recovery--Sequence of Events

Data Safety and Usability

We cannot consider data as truly safe until it has been moved off-site, as a disaster might destroy the whole building, including the original data on disk and the backup copy.

Upon a closer look, we find that data can exist in four states (see Figure 11):

- Unsafe

  As long as data remains at the primary location, it is exposed and may be lost in the event of a disaster. Unsafe data may be either:

  – Not Transferable

  This data is usually located on disk and is not ready for off-site transfer. It could be a database transaction log that has not been archived to tape, it might be a database that has not been backed up, or it might be a message that has not been queued for transmission.

  – Transferable

This is data that is ready for off-site transfer, but has not yet been transferred, such as a database backup copy on tape (sometimes called image copy). From a disaster recovery point of view, this data is also unsafe.

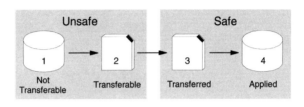

Figure 11. *Data State Model*

- Safe

  When data is transferred to another location, it is safe from any problem at the primary location.

  – Transferred

  This is data that has been taken off-site, but not applied to the backup system. Again, it could be a database image copy on tape, a database transaction log, or a message received at the backup site but not yet scheduled for processing.

  If an application is switched to the backup site, it may have to wait for the data to be applied.

  – Applied

  A backup copy of the data exists at the alternate site, and the transferred data has been applied to the copy. An example is the process of restoring a transferred database image copy onto disk, or the process of updating a database by applying a transaction log to an older version of the database. Such a process is referred to as *forward recovery*.

If an application is switched to the backup site, it can move to production work more quickly, as it may not have to wait for any data to be applied.

In a sense, this data is even safer than the "transferred" data, in that applying the data confirms that it has been backed up correctly and is useable.

Orphan Data

Assuming regular backups are taken and transported off-site, there will always be data updates that have been entered and committed before the disaster, but after the last safe backup (see Figure 10 on page 51). This data is often called orphan data.

If this data is lost in a disaster, it must somehow be re-entered or rebuilt from other sources. Note that re-entry requires access to the data source or some kind of record at the data entry point. The data may still exist on a data-entry workstation or on data entry forms. The collection and re-entry of orphan data can be time-consuming and greatly increase the recovery time.

Worse still, in some cases this data can not be recreated and is lost. Most businesses can sustain some level of data loss; however, there is pressure to make this loss as small as possible.

The amount of orphan data depends on the frequency of the backups. If data backups are taken only once a day, there will be up to one day's worth of orphan data. By increasing the frequency of backups the amount of orphan data can be reduced. In some cases this may be an acceptable and practical solution. However, many of today's online systems do not have the capacity to add more backups--especially if they require the shutting down of the online system.

Database Data: For data held in a database, which is the majority of business data, there is another option to reduce orphan data. Most DBMSs produce a log file, a continual record of all updates made to the database. Database recovery consists of restoring the latest backup of the database and then applying all the updates in the log file that have occurred since that backup was taken. If this log data can be periodically written to portable storage media (usually tape) and transported off-site, the amount of orphan data can be reduced dramatically.

Orphan data is illustrated in Figure 12. In this scenario, a backup of the database is taken early in the morning immediately following batch processing. The next backup is not scheduled until the next morning. A disaster occurs late in the day during online processing. If no logs were copied and transported off-site there would be many hours of orphan data. By copying the log data to portable storage media and transporting this data off-site, the orphan data is significantly reduced.

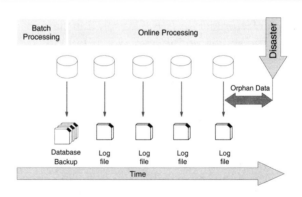

Figure 12. Using Logs to Reduce Orphan Data

Taking this one stage further, if the active log data is written off-site to a remotely attached storage device, then data loss could be almost eliminated.

Non-Database Data: When a database is not used, other methods of repeating these updates must be employed. In some cases, it may be possible to rerun the original transactions.

If this is not an option, periodic backups alone will have to be used. This may be acceptable if the data is very static, if the updates occur at regular and predictable intervals, or if some level of data loss is acceptable. In all other cases, the result will be an unacceptable data loss. This loss may prompt the migration of this data to a DBMS or the introduction of some other technique to recreate the data.

In summary, when reviewing the backup/logging needs of data, it is important to consider whether the data is recreatable, whether it is volatile, whether the updates are predictable, whether the data is important, what the acceptable window is for recovery, and how much data loss is acceptable before deciding upon the methods of backup, logging, and recovery.

Lost Data

Most disaster recovery plans will assume some loss of data. This data loss can be planned or unplanned. Planned data loss is the data loss that is inherent in the disaster recovery strategy chosen. As discussed in "Completeness of Recovery (Data Currency) versus Cost" on page 101, the amount of data that may be lost is dependent upon the solution selected and is determined by business needs. The more stringent the requirement, the higher the cost of the solution.

There is also the possibility that data will be lost inadvertently through error, either in the design of the recovery process or in its execution. The likelihood of loss due to these latter causes can be reduced by testing the process as described in "Test the Plan" on page 150.

Catch-up Data

Throughout the outage, additional transactions can be generated from the business. There may be a way to process them manually. If this is not the case, they become *catch-up data*; that is, they have to be collected and entered after the recovery, just like the orphan data.

Data Recovery

Most standard data recovery processes consist of restoring to disk the latest available backups of the data and then, where appropriate, applying any updates that have occurred since these backups were taken. In theory this is a simple process, but in practice a number of factors often cause it to be quite complex.

As the data in each installation grows and as the time available to backup the data is reduced due to online requirements, it has become increasingly difficult to back up all data as one piece. Therefore, many companies are forced into backing up different portions of their data at different times on different days.

Data recovery, therefore, involves not just restoring the data but also ensuring data consistency. Of course, not all data needs to be at the exact level of currency. For instance, the operating system (system data) can often be a week or more old and still support the applications. Even within the business data, it is unlikely that all the data has to be at exactly the same level. On the other hand, there will be some data that must be consistent if the applications are to run successfully. The dependencies between different portions of data are discussed in the following section, "Interrelationships Within the Data."

Interrelationships Within the Data

Initially, it may appear that backing up the data and making it safe are simple tasks. This is not necessarily so. Most data backup strategies are designed to handle recovery from media failure where the data will be restored to similar hardware. For disaster recovery, the recovery plan must be sufficiently flexible to recover to the alternate site. This section discusses the complexity and interdependence of data to explain why simple backup techniques may not be adequate.

File Consistency

Data is stored in a computer system as files, often referred to as data sets. Often these files are not meaningful by themselves. They have a logical relationship to other data. An example of this is a catalog that accesses a file or a database containing multiple related files.

Figure 13 shows four files that are part of one database. Each file contains a different portion of the employee information in the database. The index is used to access the employee data. Thus the business view of the employee spans all four files. These files must be backed up simultaneously to ensure a consistent view of information for all employees.

If the name file was backed up, and then an employee was added and the address file was backed up, a restore of these files would result in the address file containing information with no corresponding information in the name file. A more serious situation would occur if the index is backed up, one employee is removed and another one is added and then the remaining files are backed up. The index may now point to the incorrect employee.

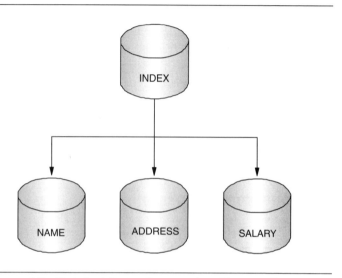

Figure 13. *Related Data Grouped to Form a Database*

Even though each file can be read (that is, there is no physical corruption of the file) the database is logically inconsistent (that is, there is logical corruption). Standard utilities exist for database managers to provide rudimentary checking of database consistency. Applications may be necessary to check the accuracy of the contents of the database. A simple program may be used to perform certain cross checks (for example, checking that totals balance).

Since database data is usually more complex in its structures and requires special consideration for backup, most DBMSs provide utilities for this purpose. Hence, interrelationships in non-database data can often be even more challenging for disaster recovery.

Whenever there are interrelationships between data, all dependent files must be backed up and recovered to a consistent point.

Business Transaction Consistency

Every disaster recovery plan must consider the business process in totality, not simply the work performed within DP. A business transaction may update information within the computing system as well as other records, such as paper or microfiche. If synchronization of this data is important, procedures must be put in place to recover all related data consistently.

A more common concern is where a single business transaction makes updates to several databases. If these databases are all controlled by the same DBMS, synchronization is reasonably straightforward. However, business transactions that access multiple DBMSs are increasingly being developed.

Data Backup Options

As discussed above, data recovery usually consists of restoring a copy of the data and applying any necessary updates. Most installations use such backup/recovery procedures today within their prime site, for the purpose of in-house recovery. When data is to be restored at a secondary data center, extra considerations apply. Hardware at both sites must be compatible. Backup data must be taken off-site quickly. Normal operations must not be overly impacted by data backup procedures.

Point-in-time Copies

Point-in-time copies back up the data as it exists at a specific instant. Traditionally, this has meant stopping the application / DBMS so that no updates can be performed, copying the data, and then restarting the application / DBMS. Based on the definitions of readiness defined in "Readiness of the Alternate Site" on page 64, point-in-time copies are typically used for periodic backup or to provide a starting point for ready-to-roll-forward implementations. Two basic types of point-in-time copies are available:

- **Logical copies** are those that back up the content of the data but not necessarily the physical format. These provide the most flexibility during recovery, as the data can be recovered to a different device type. On the other hand, a logical copy usually takes longer to create.

- **Physical copies** have historically been the simplest and fastest. With physical copies, data is copied in a device-dependent manner, usually at the volume level. This may be adequate for backup within one site, but in a second site with unlike devices, it might not be suitable. Additionally, it does not guarantee consistency within a set of files that span several volumes, and it does not support database concepts.

Online Copies

Data backup should be performed with minimal or no outage at the primary data center. To achieve this, many DBMSs now provide services that back up data while the databases are in use. The copy produced by these services is not consistent on its own. Recovery involves restoring this copy and applying to it all the updates that occurred during the backup process. This procedure creates a consistent copy. The limitation of this method is that because the recovered database is current to a point after the end of the copy operation, it is difficult to synchronize with backups of other files or databases.

Other products use a combination of software and hardware techniques to create a consistent point-in-time copy of the data as it looked at the beginning of the copy operation, while still allowing updates to the data to proceed. This technique is more suitable when multiple backups need to be synchronized.

Incremental Copies

Incremental copies are copies of data where only the changed parts of the data are copied. These copies are only useable when used together with an earlier full copy of the data. Incremental copies are used to reduce the copy time. If only a small portion of the data has changed, incremental copies can be useful. However, where significant portions of the data have changed, incremental copies may take longer than a full copy.

Copy DBMS Log Data

Log data is a collection of all the updates made to a database. These updates are written to a file by the DBMS. When this file is full, the DBMS will begin writing the updates to another log file. This process is often called a log switch. Once the switch occurs, the full log file is copied to another file called an archive log.

Data Transport and Secure Storage

The most common method of transferring disaster recovery data from the primary site to the alternate site is by copying the data to tape cartridge and transporting it manually. This data is usually moved to an off-site storage vendor, not to the alternate site.

This procedure is appropriate in many cases. However, as the pressure has increased for shorter recovery times, less data loss, and easier data management, many companies have begun to transfer data electronically.

There are three basic configurations for electronic data transfer:

- Processor to processor connection

  Data transfer typically requires software to support and manage the data.

- Processor to remote device connection

  A remote device, usually disk or tape, is channel-connected to a processor. Data written to this device is immediately transferred to the remote location. There is often a distance limitation for this type of configuration.

- Remote connection of disk controllers

  One disk controller is located remotely but connected to a disk controller at the primary site. This enables the mirroring of all updates on the primary site controller to disks on the remote controller. There is usually a trade-off between distance and performance for this type of configuration.

The decision on whether to use manual tape transport, processor to processor connection, remote devices, or

mirrored disks depends on a number of factors
including:

- The target recovery time

  The shorter the recovery time required, the more
  current the data needs to be kept. This concept of
  data currency or data *readiness* is discussed in
  "Readiness of the Alternate Site" on page 64.

- The amount of data to be transferred

  Communications bandwidth between sites can be
  expensive if large amounts of data need to be
  transferred.

- The allowable data loss

  Electronic data transfer allows the data to be moved
  off-site far more quickly than manual tape transport.
  If data loss is to be minimized, manual tape transport
  may not be adequate.

When data is transferred physically between sites or to
off-site storage, care must be exercised to ensure that
it is strictly managed. This is to safeguard against both
the loss of critical data and to keep sensitive data
secure. Consider the use of professional security
organizations to transfer the storage media.

Data transmitted electronically is usually easier to
manage and to safeguard against data loss. If very
sensitive data has to be transmitted over
communication lines, encryption techniques must be
considered. If encryption techniques are employed,
ensure that security-key management is provided at the
recovery site.

Readiness of the Alternate Site

The time between a disaster and the beginning of production work at the second site should be short. A quick recovery is possible if the second site is ready at all times, with all required hardware installed and all data at a current level.

The readiness of the recovery site is often categorized as follows:

- Cold site

    A recovery site that may be equipped with a DP infrastructure (for example, a raised floor, air conditioning, or even network connections), but with little or no DP equipment installed.

- Hot site

    A recovery site with all the required IT equipment installed.

    In many cases, this term is used to mean specifically a hot site service offered by a third party. In this book we will use the terms *commercial hot site* and *company-owned second site* to distinguish between a third party and a company-owned hot site.

There are problems associated with this terminology:

The terms *cold site* and *hot site* (and even *warm site* on some occasions) are widely used in a subjective and variable way. Also, using the above definitions, a hot site can be anything from an idle processor and disk to a live system being continuously updated and immediately ready to be used in a disaster. In addition, these terms almost never apply to any given disaster recovery strategy as a whole. An installation could, for instance, provide a hot backup for one application, while there are only warm or cold backups for the rest of the DP environment.

Therefore, these terms are useful only in a broad or comparative sense. They cannot be used to accurately describe any given disaster recovery strategy. A more precise description of the readiness of a backup site has to take the viewpoint of a particular application or piece of data. The main aspects are the backup method and the techniques used at the recovery site to manage backup data. The readiness level of an application or its data may be:

- None

    No provision is made for disaster recovery

- Periodic Backup

    At a certain time the installation takes a consistent copy of everything requiring recovery at that point and sends it to a safe location.

- Ready-to-Roll-Forward

    In addition to periodic backups, data update logs are sent to a safe location. Transport may be by physical or electronic media. Recovery will be obtained from the last log file received.

- Roll-Forward

    A *shadow* copy of the data is maintained on disk at a recovery site. Data update logs are collected there, and they are periodically applied to the shadow copy through recovery utilities. Transmission may be by physical or electronic media; however, physical transport is extremely cumbersome to manage in this case.

- Realtime-Roll-Forward

    This is similar to roll-forward, except that updates are transmitted electronically and applied at the same time they are being logged in the production site.

This *near real time* transmission and application of
log data would not impact transaction response time
at the production site.

- Realtime-Remote-Update

  This is the capability to update both the primary and
  shadow copy of data, prior to sending the transaction
  response or completing a program/task.

  This technique requires electronic data transfer.

Manage and Operate the Alternate Site

When designing the disaster recovery solution, it is
important to consider how the alternate site will be
managed and operated. This section discusses some
of the factors that influence this decision.

These factors vary depending on the nature of the
alternate site. If the alternate site is an existing data
processing site, the changes required may be small. If
the alternate site is a new site to be built, then a
completely new management infrastructure will be
required. If the alternate site is a commercial hot site,
its operation must be coordinated between the owner of
the primary site and the hot site service provider.

Options for Operating an Alternate Site

Setting up and running a recovery site has a major
effect on operations management. This section
discusses the operational issues that must be
considered when planning and implementing disaster
recovery.

In planning an alternate site for disaster recovery, you
must decide how the site is to be operated. There are
basically three options to choose from:

- No operations at the alternate site

  This will be the case if you have chosen not to run a workload at the alternate site. This could be because your alternate site is a cold site, a commercial hot site or a mobile recovery service. In this case, operations only become important at the time of the disaster.

- Alternate site unmanned, operated remotely

  An alternate site which is running a workload could be operated from the prime site. If a disaster affects the prime site, the operations staff would have to be transported to and housed at the alternate site or some other command center. The time required to transport operators to the secondary data center must then be incorporated into the time allowed for the recovery.

  Alternatively, the operations center may be remote from both the prime and secondary sites. If this is the case, and if the operations center is not affected by the disaster, transporting operations personnel is not required. Of course, the operations center would be a single point of failure for both sites and special backup arrangements have to be considered.

  In some cases, clients of commercial hot sites are running minimal systems at the hot site for the purpose of transferring data to this site electronically. These systems are either operated by the service provider or operated remotely from the prime site.

- Operations staff at both sites

  If operations staff are located at both sites, recovery will usually be simpler and faster. This option will typically require more operators and be more expensive than when they are consolidated in one place.

The first two options require implementation of a combination of remote and automated operations. If such operations are not utilized or if their use is minimal, then the third option is really the only solution.

Considerations When Assessing Options

In assessing the options for operating an alternate site, you must consider their effect on operations activities, namely:

- Processor activities, such as power on and start up
- Console interpretations and interactions
- Tape handling
- Print handling
- Environmental monitoring
- Operations planning
- Resetting control units
- Access to raised floor areas

Processor Activities

An operator is required to perform basic processor functions such as power up, restart, and shutdown. When planning for disaster recovery these functions must be considered for recovery sites that are unmanned or partially manned. Almost all of these actions may be carried out from a remote location or automated.

Console Interpretations and Interactions

The operator must read and understand messages that are displayed on the console. These messages may relate to actions such as tape mounts or special forms mounts in printers. Other message types are information, warning, and error messages which may require action by the operator.

Using current products, all console interaction can be handled remotely. In practice, however, this becomes difficult unless some level of automation is also introduced. This is because the increased message traffic and the complexity of interacting with two separate sites can easily result in mistakes, especially when one is remote.

Messages, codes, and replies at the second site should be automated using the software products available. This results in greater control in operations management. In a disaster, this control will allow for a more efficient workload switch to the recovery site. When these operations are controlled from a remote location, recovery can be achieved even more quickly, as there is no need to transport operators to the recovery site.

Tape Handling

Three options are available to allow the processing of tapes at a recovery site that is attended by only a few operators or even none. Examples are shown in Figures 14, 15, and 16.

Figure 14. *Unattended Tape Handling*

First, the use of a tape robot, like the IBM 3494 or 3495 Tape Library Dataserver, at the second site enables tapes to be mounted and dismounted automatically. This configuration is shown in Figure 14. Tape handling has traditionally been a manual process. The introduction of automated tape libraries has reduced this requirement greatly. Some manual operation is still required, for instance, to move vital backup tapes between the tape library and an off-site vault.

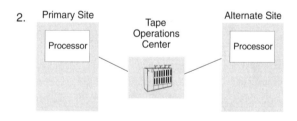

Figure 15. *Tape Handling at a Specialized Site*

The second option is to place the tape devices at a third site and connect them both to the prime site and the recovery site. This option is shown in Figure 15. This configuration has the advantage that the backup data on the tapes is held at a site that is remote to the processing sites. However, if manual tape devices are used, then tape operations personnel would still be required at this third site.

This configuration is viable if the tapes are used exclusively for backup data. If the tapes contain business data, however, the tape operations center would be a single point of failure. Any business data on tape would have to be backed up regularly and stored at yet another location.

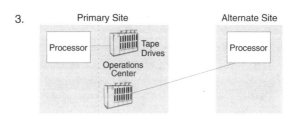

Figure 16. Tape Handling at Prime Location Only

A third option is to place the tapes and drives on the prime site in a separate secure room. They can be remotely connected to the recovery site, as shown in Figure 16. There is the obvious risk that the tape room at the prime site could be hit by a disaster that destroys the prime site completely. At worst, the organization is left without any means to recover. If this configuration is chosen, special precautions are necessary to reduce the residual risk. The secure tape room usually needs to be especially well protected against many potential disasters.

When tapes are transported between sites, operations must provide some sort of tracking system, preferably automated, that logs tapes leaving one site and arriving at another. This tracking system must also include information such as whether the data has been applied or restored at the receiving site, whether it has been reintroduced into the tape movement cycle, and its location if archived.

In addition, measures must be in place to ensure that there is no chance of confusing in-house backup tapes with off-site backup tapes, or confusing different generations of backup with each other.

The use of an automated tape library at the remote site gives more control over tracking and locating tapes and hence improves recovery procedures.

Print Handling

Printing and print distribution have been operations responsibilities for many years and have to be addressed when planning for disaster recovery. There are three main options to consider when planning the recovery of central print shops:

- Install duplicate equipment at the recovery site that would handle the daily print requirement.

- Keep available space for equipment that would be leased or purchased in a disaster.

- Secure a "recovery only" service contract, which many third party print bureau service providers are now offering.

Print distribution from a central point should also be reviewed with disaster recovery in mind, as printouts can be transported from several sites to a central point for distribution.

Remote printing should not be affected by site changes as long as printer addresses are kept the same across sites. Channel attached printers may be switched between sites using special hardware.

Many DP installations have shifted some or all of their printing from local to distributed printing across network connections. In disaster recovery mode, these printers need to be switched into the recovery configuration. See "Site Interconnection" on page 83 for details on the network connectivity issues of disaster recovery.

Environmental Monitoring

Operations is usually responsible for monitoring the computer center environment, including air conditioning, chilled water flow, humidity, and power.

If you are planning to run a data center with little or no operations staff, you must consider providing some automated environmental monitoring. In any machine room there are many types of environmental control systems: fire, smoke, water detectors, water and power supplies, emergency lighting, extinguishing systems, and so on. These elements protect life and property from damage or loss in the event of various accidents. In addition, there are the aspects of site security, access detection, and verification to consider.

Most of the controls for these systems are independent and react to different circumstances. In some cases, however, they may have some interdependencies; for example, fire detectors and extinguishing systems may connect to the air-conditioning system.

The overall specification of the environment at the secondary site is also important, as you must make sure that if you are relying on the site for backup, it is as resilient as possible. For example, it may be necessary to consider installing an uninterruptible power supply, which can minimize the impact of power surges and provide an alternative source of power in the event of power failure.

Reset Terminal Control Units

From time to time, operations is required to reset terminal control units that have become unusable for various reasons.

When planning for a secondary site that is unmanned, this action should be carefully considered. A possible solution would be to move the terminal control units to an area that is easily accessible to technical service personnel but at the same time secure from unauthorized tampering. A second solution would be to utilize available hardware technology and install these control units at the remote operator site.

Access to Raised Floor Areas

Operations has also been responsible for controlling access to the computer room. Technicians and various other service personnel will need access during recovery periods and may have to be escorted and assisted by operations personnel. This responsibility could involve changes to the existing access control mechanisms when recovery personnel are required to work at the second site.

Automated Operations

Automated operations means the automation of tasks traditionally performed by computer operators. This can be accomplished in many ways using both hardware and software products. Refer to *Disaster Recovery Library S/390 Technology Guide* (see "International Technical Support Organization Publications" on page 193) for further discussion on the importance of automation to disaster recovery planning and the implementation of automated operations using the hardware and software product offerings.

When moving from one to two or more data centers, automation of operations can assist in limiting the number of operations staff required by improving operator productivity. Automation reduces the repetitive tasks to a minimum and allows the operations staff to concentrate on the more demanding work of problem determination and solution. In addition, tools that provide the automation also provide improved facilities for the operations staff.

Automation also formalizes many of the operational procedures that have become accepted through practice rather than design. Automatic recovery actions can also be incorporated when automating operations. After a disaster, automation can be even more important in order to speed up the recovery process. However, even where systems and recovery processes are highly automated, good documentation is required that still allows manual operations. Things can go wrong; this is true especially after a disaster.

Without some level of automation, remote site operation may be impossible to implement, and the disaster recovery strategy will significantly increase the complexity of operations. Automated operations should be considered for all sites within the organization to provide the following benefits:

- To provide a structured operations environment. This will help reduce the recovery time of systems in a disaster recovery situation.

- To increase operator productivity through the suppression of unnecessary messages from the console display and by automating repetitive and complex tasks.

- To reduce or eliminate human errors and inaccuracies. This could have a direct bearing on system availability after a disaster has occurred. It may be impossible to recover complex workloads without some level of automation.

- To minimize the cost of running two or more data centers.

Operations Culture at Remote Site

When an operator-occupied second site is used, there are several requirements one must plan for. Operations personnel in the secondary center must be kept current with advances and changes in workload or product operation in the primary center. This can be accomplished by:

- Rotating the operators between the prime and secondary centers
- Keeping comprehensive, up-to-date operating instructions, workload procedures, and automation documentation
- Keeping a softcopy and a hardcopy of the complete disaster recovery plan
- Splitting the production workloads between the primary and secondary sites

Additional Considerations

The following supply and general items should be considered for every recovery center:

- Additional supplies of special form-printing stationary
- Additional supplies of private/scratch tapes/cartridges
- A fully stocked, up-to-date manual library
- Additional storage areas for tapes and stationery
- Additional rest areas
- Additional parking facilities for standby vehicles
- Physical access to the building for recovery staff

In the case of a commercial hot site, required forms, supplies, and manuals should be kept at an off-site storage facility.

Description of the Recovery Configuration

This component of the design covers the alternate site (location, hardware, and software), the interconnections between the primary and alternate sites, and the way in which the network will be connected to the alternate site.

Distance between Prime Site and Alternate Site

If a fire is the only kind of disaster to worry about, two sites can be as close as two machine rooms in the same building, isolated from each other only by a fire-proof wall. However, disasters may affect more than a single machine room or building. The disaster scope may be such that a whole area or even several cities are affected. Therefore, a greater distance between DP sites results in greater security against any wide-spread disaster.

However, great distance has its price in other terms such as interconnection cost, business relocation effort and cost, and so on. With current technology, it is neither easy nor cheap to interconnect two sites that are hundreds of miles apart at a bandwidth high enough to keep large amounts of data at both sites fully synchronized.

A moderate distance, for example, up to 20 km, gives less protection against wide-spread disasters, but has several advantages:

- High interconnection bandwidth
- Low interconnection cost
- Easy business relocation in case of a disaster
- Realtime-remote-update through high bandwidth interconnections
- Combine in-house backup and disaster backup

These aspects are discussed in detail in the following section.

Note: The degree of risk associated with moderate distance alternate sites varies greatly from region to region and country to country.

Advantages of Moderate Distance Interconnection

With state-of-the-art interconnection technology, it is possible to effectively interconnect two sites at a moderate distance from each other. The advantages include:

- High interconnection bandwidth

  High bandwidth, in this context, means more than a single link in the megabit or gigabit range. It means dozens or hundreds of links of that kind, especially when considering remote attachment of tape and disk drives.

- Low interconnection cost

  In general, the cost of interconnections is a function of the distance covered.

  The cost of connections of the magnitude just described may be prohibitive over a long distance. Costs can be very reasonable, however, over short distances, especially when contained within a company's own campus.

- Easy business relocation in case of a disaster

  If a network connection is all the users need, then the DP site may be relocated anywhere. If, however, there is a great deal of physical interaction with the central DP site, such as diskette or magnetic tape exchange, central printing, or OCR processing, this business might not function if the DP site is a hundred miles away. Also, long-term relocation of the DP personnel can be a major problem. In these cases, a short distance to the recovery site can be an important requirement.

- Realtime-remote-update through high bandwidth interconnections

  Advanced backup strategies, especially realtime-remote-update or disk shadowing, can prolong transaction response time. Therefore, they require high bandwidth, high performance interconnections. With some of these technologies, interconnection distance also affects performance. To keep the response time impact of such technologies at a minimum, it is often necessary to choose a recovery site at a moderate distance.

- Combining in-house backup and disaster backup

  Many DP environments have to maintain two separate sets of backup copies of their data. One set is kept at the primary site and is required for in-house recovery, for instance, to rebuild a database in the case of a permanent disk I/O error. The second set of backup copies is required for disaster recovery. It should therefore be taken off-site as soon as it is created.

  In many cases, the database system must be taken down during the backup process. The time available to do this can be very limited. Therefore, running and maintaining two redundant backup processes may be a major problem.

A solution to this problem is to use remote tape for backup. Tape drives could be physically located at the recovery site and connected to the prime site using extended channels. In this case, only one set of backup tapes is required. Through the remote tape drives, these tapes are immediately available for in-house recovery as well as for remote recovery in the event of a disaster.

Which Distance Is Right for You?

The distance between sites is a key decision, and this decision should be based on the results of detailed risk analysis and impact analysis exercises, as described in "Determine What the Business Requires" on page 17. The key influencing factors are the scope of disasters that are to be covered and the recovery requirements of the business processes.

Configuration Overview

A description of all hardware and software resources required at the alternate site is a central and basic part of the design. Based on the application and data recovery needs you have established, you can now define the required resources. If workload is going to be split across two sites, then this also needs to be taken into consideration when designing the recovery configuration. See "Workload Distribution across Two Sites" on page 90 for a detailed discussion on workload distribution.

Recovery Capacity

In designing the alternate site, it is vital that the resources meet the capacity and performance requirements of the organization's critical workload.

When planning for disaster recovery, you may decide to allow the entire critical application workload, or a subset of that workload, to operate in a degraded mode; that is, to reduce the cost of facilities and resources that would be required to operate the workload at maximum performance levels, fewer computer resources are made available for disaster recovery purposes. Some organizations, though, are not able to tolerate a performance degradation to any of their critical workload in disaster recovery mode.

Both options highlight the need for service level agreements to be defined for disaster recovery operation. Designers of the alternate site must ensure that they provide sufficient computer resources to meet these service level agreements.

You must also take conventional application growth into account when planning the disaster site. Capacity planners usually provide a capacity buffer at the prime site so that applications can grow at the forecasted rate. Similar capacity provisions may also be required at the recovery site.

Your capacity projections should include the critical workload to be recovered and the capacity required during the recovery itself. Early in the recovery, you may be running some of your recovered critical applications as well as still performing data restores and database recoveries, and re-entering orphan and catch-up data. For a short period, typically the second or third days, you may require extra capacity.

Remember that the defined critical application workload has a time dependency. That is, immediately after a disaster occurs, the critical applications must be recovered. However, after a period of time has elapsed, many more applications may be deemed to be part of the critical workload. Capacity planners must ensure that they plan for this. "Determine What the Business Requires" on page 17 describes the *critical workload* in more detail.

Dependence on Specific Components

The planned resource for the recovery site must include a hardware and software configuration that meets the specific requirements of each application defined in the critical workload. If an application at the prime site requires a specific feature for operation, then that feature must exist at the backup site as well. If applications are device-dependent, then compatible devices must be configured at the recovery site.

In some cases, applications may depend on the availability of special or custom-built equipment. In this case, a decision must be made as to whether the equipment will be duplicated at the recovery site or whether it will be acquired or rebuilt at the time of a disaster. For some equipment, rebuilding will mean an unacceptable delay, and therefore the only choice will be to maintain duplicate hardware.

Availability of Resources

In addition to sizing the resources that are required for recovery, you will need to determine the availability requirements for these resources.

For example, if your most critical application needs to be up in six hours and recovery takes five, then you need to ensure that the receiving disk for that application is available almost immediately. This would be impossible if the receiving disk was being used for development, as it would take some time to back up the data and re-initialize the disk. In this case, you may need resources dedicated to disaster recovery.

The availability requirements of the recovery resources are driven by the recovery time and data readiness needs of the critical applications.

Site Interconnection

The prime and secondary sites do not need to be interconnected for disaster recovery. Data on tape, for instance, may be regularly carried to the recovery site. Still, in order to provide the best possible data protection as well as the quickest possible takeover in the case of a disaster, data must be transmitted off-site as fast and frequently as possible. This is best achieved by using high-bandwidth interconnection technology to connect remote disk or tape devices through extended channels. Apart from cost, distance may be a limiting factor here. Although emerging technology may extend this capability in the future, it is probable that the highest bandwidth interconnection technology will always imply a certain distance limitation.

Interconnection Options

Remote site interconnection can be categorized in four increments, as illustrated in Figure 17.

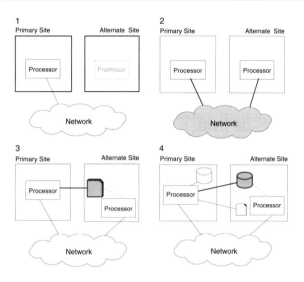

Figure 17. Site Interconnection

These interconnection *models*, although not an exhaustive list, depict four typical increments of site interconnection technology:

1. Remote site not interconnected

   Although not a common practice, it is possible for the recovery site to not be connected to the prime site. A major problem here is the time it takes after a disaster to establish a network connection with the users. It is also not easy to test the takeover without an interconnection.

   To facilitate disaster recovery, backup data on tapes is physically transported to the recovery site. This method of data transportation has certain advantages:

   • It is well-suited to very large amounts of data, such as complete databases or disk packs.

- It is suitable for any information stored on paper. There will always be a need to regularly ship documents to the second site.
- It is relatively cheap.

However, there are some disadvantages:

- The data is "unsafe" as long as the media are queued for transport. Therefore, there is a great potential for data loss in case of a disaster (see "Orphan Data" on page 53).
- Third parties must be involved, and this introduces potential management and security issues.
- The tape volumes must be tracked and then recycled at some point.

2. Network connection

Most traditional networks are designed for transaction workload and server access and therefore rely on medium bandwidth connection lines. Such a network allows some inter-site data transmission as well as user access to the recovery site. However, in most cases it does not eliminate the need for physical data transport. Network connection provides a means for moving data to the second site as soon as it is made transferable. This avoids the disadvantages of physical transportation previously mentioned.

Data may even be received by the second site at the transaction level (for example, to maintain a remote mirror copy of a database).

Although data may be received at a transaction level, the remote data update is likely to be designed to take place asynchronously in order not to degrade the response time. The network is also well-suited for the transmission of system management and system maintenance data.

Certain limitations have to be considered, however:

- Active DP equipment is required at both the sending and the receiving sites.
- Telecommunication lines have a limited data rate when compared to large system I/O channels.

3. Remote tape

Remote tape has the advantage of placing backup data in a safe state without passing through an unsafe intermediate period, during which it is transferable (see "Data Safety and Usability" on page 51). It usually requires a transmission bandwidth in excess of traditional networks. Furthermore, it facilitates the integration of in-house backup and disaster backup (see "Advantages of Moderate Distance Interconnection" on page 78).

4. Remote disk

Remote disk may be used to maintain backup data in a safe and usable state (see "Data Safety and Usability" on page 51). In other words, it allows remote copies of vital data to be maintained at a very current level, thus providing warm or even hot backup (see "Readiness of the Alternate Site" on page 64).

Communications Network Design

There are two components in the network design for disaster recovery. The first is the capability to connect the network to the alternate site in the event of a disaster or for testing. The second is the possible network connection between the sites to allow data transfer. Although these components are logically separate, they may share the same network infrastructure.

- Network connection in the event of a disaster

In the event of disaster, the network has to be connected to the alternate site. This can be achieved by a number of different methods, including using dial-up lines, switching lines at the time of the disaster, or having lines permanently installed at the alternate site.

The line capacity required following the disaster must be analyzed carefully. The movement of the workload to the alternate site can cause major shifts in network traffic. Users may change from local to remote attachment, and former remote users may require significantly different transmission routes through the network.

In many cases, costs will prohibit the duplication of the entire production network, and in actual fact it may be necessary to recover only a portion of the production network based on the critical workload and locations included in the scope of the recovery plan.

Some level of network connectivity is also required to test recovery at the alternate site. For much of the testing this will be a subset of the network required for a disaster; however, the full network activation needs to be tested periodically to ensure that it will work in a disaster.

The network requirements will be based on the analysis of the application recovery requirements as discussed in "Determine the Data Processing Requirements" on page 31.

- Connection between sites for data transfer

  The disaster recovery configuration may include the electronic transfer of data through a network connection between the prime and alternate sites. This may include:

  - Remote operation

    Operation of one or both sites may be remotely controlled, which can cause a substantial additional message flow over the network.

  - System and application changes

    It is desirable that all systems and application software at both sites be kept synchronized. A reasonable way of shipping change data to a remote site is to use the network.

  - Systems management

    Most systems management tasks require the network. For example, in addition to the change data just described, appropriate change management data has to be exchanged.

  - Database backup copies

    If complete files or database backup copies are to be sent across the network, it will require extremely high capacity transmission links.

  - Database transaction logs

    In order to facilitate a roll-forward process at the recovery site (see "Readiness of the Alternate Site" on page 64), database transaction logs must be sent periodically to the recovery site. If the network is chosen as the transmission medium, this will cause an additional network load.

  - Remote tapes or disks

    As illustrated in Figure 17 on page 84, tape or disk devices may be placed at the alternate site, connected to the primary site through remote channels or channel extensions. In addition to the wide area network, such channel extensions must be part of the network design for disaster recovery.

A network design that provides a disaster recovery capability must have the following properties:

- Network access for both sites

  This is required for both workload takeover and periodic testing.

- Uses separate gateways for each site

  In the context of disaster recovery, a network gateway machine is a single point of failure. For disaster recovery a second gateway must exist, and the two gateways cannot be located close to each other. The goal is that the recovery site does not lose its network access when a disaster occurs at the location of the prime site's gateway.

- Both sites must be able to control the network

  Large networks, although they may connect several sites, are typically controlled from one location. A provision must exist to move the network control function to another site in the event of a disaster at the controlling location.

- Isolated external paths

  If two sites exist each has its own network gateway, a single point of failure may exist in the external connection between the gateways and a public telephone interchange facility. Ideally, both gateways should be connected to separate public telephone interchange facilities. Note that this requirement may be difficult to meet if both sites are close together.

- Alternate paths for all locations

  The network topology should provide alternate paths between host locations and all remote user locations. Typically, this is a requirement for high availability, and, as such, it is often fulfilled even where no explicit disaster recovery strategy exists.

- Automatic path switching

Wherever path switching is required in the event of disaster recovery, it should take place automatically or under central control. Remote users are usually not trained or sufficiently experienced to perform this task reliably.

Workload Distribution across Two Sites

If a company's second site is to be used for disaster recovery, you will need to decide how best to allocate all of your workload across the two sites.

Spare Recovery Resources on Call

The simplest option is to run the entire workload at the prime site and ensure that there is sufficient resource ready at the recovery site. This solution is illustrated in Figure 18.

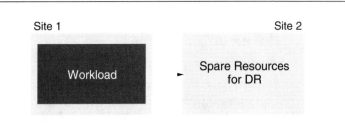

Figure 18. One-Way Site Recovery Relationship

This solution has the benefit that recovery is relatively straightforward. In addition, the recovery site could also run a copy of the prime site software, ready to take over immediately in the event of a disaster. In some cases, this type of strategy may be required due to business recovery requirements.

In most cases, however, a business cannot justify an idle recovery site.

Note: In essence, this is what third party recovery service providers offer--sufficient recovery resources available when required (see "Select the Recovery Site" on page 106).

Split the Workload

A more viable strategy, shown in Figure 19, is to separate the non-critical workload and run it at the recovery site. In some cases, this may mean a split of development and production; in other cases, some business functions may be more vital than others, enabling a split by application.

In this setting, if the recovery site suffers a disaster, the critical workload stays intact. Only if a disaster occurs at the prime site is disaster recovery necessary. This is a more acceptable solution as it reduces the amount of idle capacity. Typically, the non-critical workload is greater than the critical workload, and therefore some amount of idle capacity will be available at the recovery site. Assuming the non-critical workload is not required in the case of a disaster, no spare capacity is required at the prime site. Note, however, that in general, all workload becomes critical as an outage continues and therefore some provision for recovery must be made. For further discussion see "Recovery Priority" on page 28.

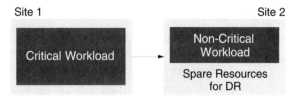

Figure 19. Mutual Recovery Relationship

Even if the non-critical workload can be displaced, time may be required to back up the data and re-initialize the disk volumes.

A variation of this workload split is shown in Figure 20. The critical workload is split between site 1 and site 2. In the event of a disaster, some part of the critical workload would always be affected, while the rest of the critical workload could stay intact. Note that advanced database system functions, such as function shipping or distributed data, could interfere with this goal. Therefore, from a disaster recovery point of view, the important aspect in application design is to make sure that even if mutual dependencies exist between the two parts of the workload, they are of a magnitude so that a failure of one site does not affect the other one.

This approach may be required when portions of the critical and non-critical workloads are difficult to separate.

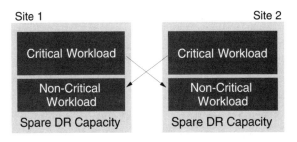

Figure 20. *Critical Workload Split-Mutual Recovery*

When workload splitting is necessary, the split should be designed so that both sites are independent. A failure of one site should not immediately affect operation at the other. This approach requires, for instance, that all data needed for applications at site 1 is located at site 1, while all data for applications at site 2 is at site 2.

Split the Critical Workload

Dividing the critical workload in a practical but useful way is often a complex activity and is highly dependent on the nature of each installation. It is beyond the scope of this book to fully cover this topic; however, some points to be considered are discussed below.

Best-Fit: An apparently simple approach is a *best fit* division of the workload by application. In this case, the critical applications would be separated into two groups requiring similar capacities to run. In a static situation, this is quite simple. However, the workload in most organizations grows unevenly, which requires constant adjustment of the workload division.

This means an increase in monitoring to ensure that the available capacity for critical applications at both data centers is adequate.

In addition, applications are often related to each other through data and processing, making it difficult in many cases to separate them. A good knowledge of these applications is vital to enable such a split.

Interrelationships with Non-Critical Workloads: If the purpose of the split is to provide mutual backup, it makes sense to divide the critical workload between the two data centers and then put the remaining workload wherever it will fit.

Sometimes, part of the less critical workload is dependent on critical databases or applications. In such cases, the location of the less critical applications is determined by that of the critical application. Hence, an analysis of application dependencies must be part of determining which of the critical applications goes to which data center.

Split the Network: In some cases, an application is run in both data centers for different subsets of users. Generally, this implies a network split.

The network might be split in a number of ways:

- 50/50

  The users are divided, more or less at random, across the two data centers.

- Geographically

  Each data center services the users in one or more particular geographic locations.

- Alternate geographically

  Geographically adjacent users are assigned to alternate data centers. This means that, in the event of one data centers failing, the whole area is still covered but the number of users, services is halved.

- Random geographically

Users are selected at random for assignment to one of the data centers. Similar to alternate geographically, in the event of a failure at one data center, the service area is still covered and approximately 50% of the users are still serviced.

- Functionally

  Users are selected by business function for assignment to one or other of the data centers. Thus, all the users of one function would be serviced by one data center and all the users of another function by the other data center.

Other Considerations

Splitting the workload across the two sites is usually necessary; however, there are drawbacks:

- Some "idle" capacity will almost invariably be required because it is almost impossible to split the workload evenly or proportionally across the two sites.

- Where critical workload is split across multiple sites, dual disaster recovery plans are required--one for each site. Because these plans must interact, the complexity is greatly increased.

- The operation and management of two active sites is more complex.

In general, the discussions in this book reflect a one-way relationship between a *prime site* and an associated *recovery site*, as shown in Figure 18 on page 90. Although this is a simplification, it is a reasonable approach because in any single disaster situation, recovery will only occur in one direction. The principles derived for this approach are easily extendable to the "mutual recovery" situation.

Application Programming Considerations

The implementation of disaster recovery usually requires few, if any, changes to application programming. However, certain programming and database design standards should be considered when developing new applications, to make disaster recovery easier and more transparent.

You could also consider rewriting or updating existing applications as part of the implementation of the disaster recovery solution. The cost of doing this would have to be assessed against the benefits that would be gained.

Application Design

Where recoverability after a disaster in an important requirement, applications should be designed with disaster recovery in mind. Transportability is important. Complex interfaces and linkages with other applications should be avoided. Try to make each application as autonomous or self-contained as possible. Note that these design objectives are in conflict with traditional database and application design approaches, which call for non-redundant databases, and an integration of systems and applications. For each application, there is a trade-off to be made between these conflicting design approaches, based on the particular application's underlying business requirements.

Changes to applications that will affect recovery, capacity, and performance should be communicated through change management channels.

To minimize the potential for lost data and to provide faster recovery, applications should be designed so that commits of data are performed as frequently as possible.

Operator communication to process the workload should be eliminated or kept to a minimum.

Ideally, all application data should be on disk. Tape is best used as a backup media, not as storage for application data. However, many organizations still have some traditional batch applications that use generations of master files on tape. Disaster recovery for tape applications is difficult, and the risk of losing the most recent generation of these files in the event of a disaster cannot be easily eliminated. If possible, these applications should be changed to use disk files instead.

Online applications have to be adaptable to the re-entry of orphan data and the entry of recovery data. Applications should be able to accept and process bulk transactions as well as online transactions.

Development of any disaster recovery procedures that are unique to an application should be considered an integral component in the development of the application. Similarly, testing the disaster recovery procedures should be considered an integral component in testing the application.

Database Design

Databases should be designed so that they are as autonomous as possible. They should be self-contained and consist of small, transferable partitions. Avoid the corporate-wide database, which contains every possible piece of data and occupies so many disk volumes that moving it becomes virtually impossible.

When designing a database, avoid the classic case of a single transaction updating several database management subsystems in realtime mode, as recovery of this transaction type requires complex techniques.

At each site there is a trade-off between these guidelines and other design requirements. However, if the disaster recovery strategy is important to an organization, the previously mentioned factors must be considered carefully in the design.

Program Naming Conventions

Each application programming team manager should ensure that each program is named according to a standard convention. This convention should ensure that no two programs are given the same name.

Decision Criteria

In summary, there are many conflicting objectives when designing a disaster recovery solution. Consequently, an individual solution is always a compromise, and there is no single solution or recommendation that fits all DP environments.

Balancing out the four major decision criteria, as shown in Figure 21, can help you find the solution for your DP environment.

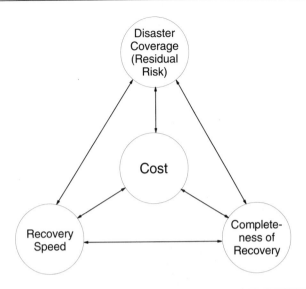

Figure 21. *Decision Criteria for an Individual Disaster Recovery Design*

The decision criteria are:

- Cost of the disaster recovery solution
- Disaster coverage (residual risk)
- Speed of recovery
- Completeness of recovery (data currency)

Between any two of these four criteria, there is a certain conflict, and therefore, some trade-off must be found. The resulting six relationships are discussed in the following sections.

Cost of the Disaster Recovery Solution

The cost of an individual solution must be in reasonable proportion to the business value of DP as a whole. In other words, do not spend more on your disaster recovery strategy than the financial loss you would suffer from a disaster. However, if a total loss of DP facilities makes it impossible for your business to operate at all, a working disaster recovery strategy might justify very high investments.

The total cost of a disaster recovery strategy consists of three components:

1. Initial cost

   This is the cost of developing a disaster recovery strategy, acquiring resources for disaster recovery (for example, building a second site), and developing appropriate recovery procedures.

2. Ongoing cost

   This is the cost of maintaining the ability to recover. It includes, for example, maintaining a given percentage of spare capacity as well as the continual expansion and testing of recovery procedures.

3. Cost in case of a disaster

   Very seldom will the resources required for all applications be available at the time of the disaster. Instead, only the most important applications are recovered immediately. Eventually, however, many additional resources may have to be acquired to meet the capacity requirements of the full workload. To the extent that this is not covered by insurance, it can be a substantial cost factor.

Disaster Coverage (Residual Risk) versus Cost

Assuming a given recovery strategy, you will find that a greater distance between sites gives better protection against wide-spread disasters (see "Distance between Prime Site and Alternate Site" on page 77). However, greater distance will increase cost in many areas, such as:

- Interconnection cost
- Transportation cost
- Operation and management cost

Speed of Recovery versus Cost

Fast recovery requires a warm or hot backup strategy. Due to the additional hardware resources, recovery procedure development, and testing efforts required, a warm backup solution is more expensive than cold backup, and a hot backup solution is still more expensive.

Completeness of Recovery (Data Currency) versus Cost

A similar argument holds for the problem of recovery completeness. If you can afford to lose a certain amount of recent transaction data through a disaster, a cold or moderately warm backup solution might suffice (in this case, it is up to the individual users to re-enter any transactions that occurred after the last backup was taken). If, however, no data loss can be tolerated, a hot backup solution or a provision to constantly transfer transaction data off-site is required. Both solutions increase cost.

Completeness of Recovery versus Recovery Speed

Getting databases up-to-date after a disaster takes some time. The more current the database has to be before users are allowed to resume their work, the longer the down-time will be from a user's perspective. In other words, disaster recovery can be either fast or complete, but typically not both.

Recovery Speed versus Disaster Coverage

With channel extension it is possible to implement a hot backup solution at a reasonable cost. However, as there is often a practical distance limitation for this kind of interconnection technology, the coverage against wide-spread disasters might not be as good as you would like (see "Distance between Prime Site and Alternate Site" on page 77).

Disaster Coverage versus Completeness of Recovery

Similarly, a channel-extension-based hot backup solution can provide excellent completeness of recovery. The limited disaster coverage due to the distance limitations is again the trade-off to be considered.

Select Products to Match the Design

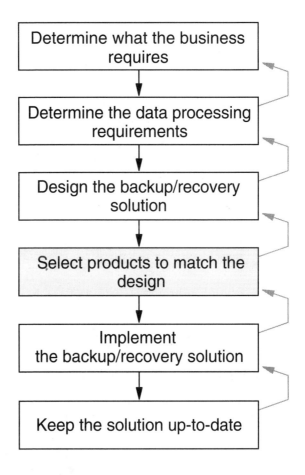

Determine what the business requires

↓

Determine the data processing requirements

↓

Design the backup/recovery solution

↓

Select products to match the design

↓

Implement the backup/recovery solution

↓

Keep the solution up-to-date

Once you have built a design of the disaster recovery solution, you can select the products that are required to implement that solution. You can then estimate the cost of disaster recovery for your organization.

The disaster recovery design that has been developed up to this point is a *logical* design. It describes the way the recovery solution will function, but it does not include an exact specification of the components that make it up. Product selection is intentionally excluded from the design to allow the initial design to be determined by the user requirements and not by the capabilities of the products. This is an important design principle.

However, it is often practical to develop the initial design with some knowledge of the available products, to avoid asking for a function for which no product exists or a product with operational restrictions. For instance, a design that specified synchronous mirroring of disks over 20 km or 200 km would result in quite different products with different performance characteristics, Therefore, some knowledge of the capabilities of the available products ensures that the resultant design is practical.

Note that to the fullest extent possible, your business requirements should determine the disaster plan independent of product selection.

Product Selection

Product selection is the process of choosing a set of products that can be used together to enable the implementation of your disaster recovery design. A product in this context is any component of the solution that needs to be bought or developed. Hardware and software are products, as is the alternate site or recovery service you plan to use and the manpower required to develop and operate the solution.

In some cases, there will be a required function in the design that is matched by only one available product. In other cases there may be no products which exactly match the requirements. When this occurs, you will need to assess the requirement to determine whether this function should be developed in-house or dropped from the design, or whether the design needs to be reworked. As previously mentioned, this situation should be avoided for the major functions of the design by endeavoring to include only functions that are known to be available.

Hardware and Software Selection

The hardware and software products you select will be highly dependent on the processing platform of the prime site. Although the functional requirements for backup and recovery are very similar across platforms, available tools and their functionalities vary greatly. It is not within the scope of this book to describe the products that support disaster recovery across all platforms. However, some of the main S/390 products that support disaster recovery are described briefly in Appendix A, "System/390 Disaster Recovery Products" on page 159 and covered more fully in *Disaster Recovery Library S/390 Technology Guide* (see "International Technical Support Organization Publications" on page 193).

Software Issues

When planning a disaster recovery site, you must ensure that any contractual agreements with suppliers of software products enable those products to be restored or run continuously at the alternate site. Some products may require additional software licenses for the second site.

Certain software products verify the processor serial number before executing. These products have to be adapted when relocating them to a processor at a different site. Assess these needs and ensure that they are highlighted in the disaster recovery plan.

Select the Recovery Site

Choosing a type of alternate site may be the most important decision you make. The alternate site need not be owned by your organization. You could use professional service providers for disaster recovery, or you could have an agreement with another company to use their DP equipment in the case of a disaster. The possible approaches include:

- Alternate site owned by your organization

  Many companies utilize data processing facilities located across multiple sites. The original reason for multiple sites may have been geographical or historical, but in any case, multiple DP sites offer a convenient infrastructure to support disaster recovery.

  If a company's second site is to be used for disaster recovery, it is vital that the distribution of workload across the sites is reviewed. This topic is discussed further in "Workload Distribution across Two Sites" on page 90.

- Third Party Recovery Service

  This approach is similar to insurance; that is, for a periodic fee and as defined in a contract, a professional recovery service provider will supply disaster recovery resources if the need arises. Such facilities are typically shared by several subscribers.

  This approach is generally far lower in cost and allows the utilization of the technical and administrative support as well as the coordination skills of the service provider.

  Many recovery service providers offer mobile recovery services in addition to the traditional "fixed" recovery sites. These mobile recovery services vary from an agreement to transport PC equipment to a fully functional large systems processing environment contained in a truck or trailer and driven to an agreed location in the event of a disaster.

IBM offers this service, called "Business Recovery Services," in various countries. This service provides a recovery site infrastructure, network resources, and a predetermined amount of DP equipment in case of a disaster. It also includes optional technical assistance for all aspects of disaster recovery from risk and impact analysis, plan development and maintenance, to support for ongoing testing and maintenance of recovery procedures.

- Mutual agreement between disaster recovery partners

  Two organizations agree to act as the recovery site for each other in the event of a disaster. This low-cost strategy may be viable in some environments, but has serious drawbacks and risks in many cases:

  – A disaster could occur at the worst possible time - when the other organization has peak load or problems of its own.

  – Most DP sites are unlikely to have much idle resource available. Consequently, such agreements are of questionable value for large companies who would need significant resources in the case of a disaster.

  – It is difficult to ensure that day-to-day changes at each site do not compromise the ability of the other organization to recover.

  – Most DP departments are not set up to allow another organization to suddenly arrive and recover their production workload. Given that recoveries are intense activities, the convergence of the two operations in the same location could cause problems for both organizations.

– Testing the recovery strategy is very difficult. Verbal agreements in this area are generally useless. If this is your chosen approach, a formal agreement must be developed; however, ensuring that all contingencies are covered may mean a very complex contract.

The choice of approach depends on a number of factors. One of the most important is cost. The least expensive disaster recovery solution may be to use a mutual agreement with another organization; however, as discussed, this is typically a high-risk option. The use of a recovery service is usually far less expensive than building your own second site. On the other hand, if you already have a suitable second data processing site, the costs to develop it for disaster recovery may be very low.

The use of a company's second site for disaster recovery usually means some level of redundant resources installed. In addition, it is often difficult to schedule sufficient testing time in such a situation, as testing impacts the day-to-day processing at the recovery site. On the other hand, using a recovery service may introduce greater complexity in managing the disaster recovery strategy due to the involvement of an external organization. In many cases, there is a limit to the size and complexity of DP environments that can be covered by such services.

The approaches also differ in the availability they offer to the recovery resources. If a company's second site is used, there may be a need to backup and remove workload and data already running on the system before recovery can proceed. If a recovery service is used, availability will depend on the details of the contract but typically includes some small delay to allow for site preparation. The mobile recovery service obviously introduces a delay in recovery due to the transport time.

The decision on ownership of the alternate site is clearly influenced by recovery requirements that have been determined. Do you need the site for disaster recovery immediately after the disaster occurs, or can there be a delay? How far apart do the sites need to be? How should the sites be interconnected?

Consider Product Quality

In "Decision Criteria" on page 98, we discussed the main trade-offs that need to be made when determining the most suitable solution. When you reach the stage of selecting products, another factor becomes relevant: product quality. Quality in this context means the degree to which you can be confident that this product will perform the required task. This is not a simple decision, as quality is difficult to measure without testing the product. However, there are a number of indicators that may give a higher degree of confidence in one product over another, all other things being equal:

- The reputation of the supplier
- The level of support offered for the product
- Availability of source code
- Proven versus new
- Simple versus complex
- Available versus unannounced
- Standard versus custom-built
- Conventional versus innovative

- Hardware versus software versus hardware and software
- Operating system code versus application code

What Does the Backup/Recovery Solution Cost?

Once the disaster recovery design has been developed and product selection is complete, you can determine the cost of the recovery solution. This cost should include all components of the solution, namely:

- Hardware
- Software
- Network
- Alternate site
- Effort to implement
- Effort to maintain

To determine which one of a number of potential solutions to pursue further, approximate cost estimations based on high level designs is sufficient. If the cost is to be determined accurately, much more detail is needed in the design and product selection.

After determining the cost of your disaster recovery solution, you need to compare it with the cost and risk of disaster. The cost of the solution must be in proportion to the cost and risk of a disaster. The risk analysis and the projected cost to the business of an outage are derived from the business requirements analysis discussed in "Determine What the Business Requires" on page 17. There is no simple methodology for this comparison. A disaster may not be highly likely in your area but may have a major impact if it does occur. What are you willing to invest to protect against such an occurrence?

In many cases, management will have a reasonably clear idea of the maximum investment it is willing to make in disaster recovery even before any solution design is done. If this is the case, it is often useful to use this figure as a guide during the design phase. That is, it may be a waste of effort and time to develop a detailed design for a solution that costs many times what the organization is willing to spend. On the other hand, it may be useful to develop a high level design just to demonstrate the cost of what the business really requires.

Often there is the need to compare alternative solutions. The shorter the required recovery time, the higher the cost of implementation and maintenance of the solution. Recovery is usually cheap or fast, but not both, as shown in Figure 22. (In practice, this curve will tend to be a series of steps rather than a smooth curve due to the incremental costs of different solutions.)

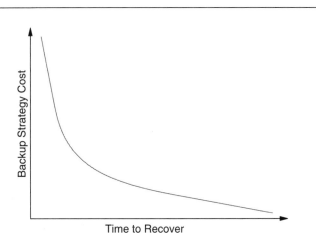

Figure 22. *Disaster Recovery Strategy: Cost and Recovery Time*

This curve can be overlaid with the cost versus outage curve illustrated in Figure 5 on page 27. (Note that to give a valid comparison, the cost versus outage curve must be the sum of the curves for *all* the business processes covered by this solution.) It is then possible to define a *cost/time-window*, in which the recovery solution should exist (see Figure 23).

Although the curves just described are very useful in the design of a suitable disaster recovery strategy, they are only estimates and should not be seen as implying more accuracy than they represent.

Of course, in deciding on the solution, the acceptable risk and other cost factors must also be considered. The cost of the required solution may be high while the probability of a certain disaster may be very low. A business decision may be made in this case to implement a less complete solution and accept the risk, as discussed in "Decision Criteria" on page 98.

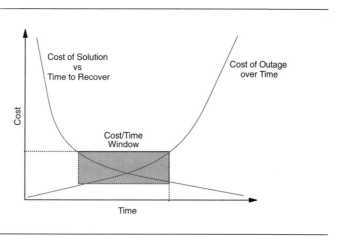

Figure 23. *Cost of DR Strategy versus Cost of Outage*

Develop a Detailed Design

In most cases, a high level design and cost estimate is sufficient to determine the appropriate solution. At some stage in the design process however it may be necessary to develop a detailed design because accurate cost and effort estimates are needed to decide between alternate options. A detailed design can be very time consuming and should only be completed when there is a strong indication that this is the preferred solution.

With a decision made on which option is most appropriate, the design can be refined to include detail on the functions, processes, and products to be bought and/or developed. At this stage it is difficult to separate detailed design from implementation in that some of the detailed design will be done prior to implementation while much of it will be performed as part of the solution implementation.

Implement the Backup/Recovery Solution

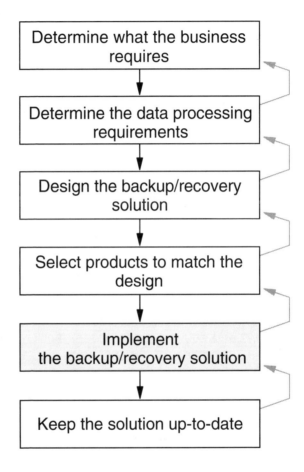

Determine what the business requires

Determine the data processing requirements

Design the backup/recovery solution

Select products to match the design

Implement the backup/recovery solution

Keep the solution up-to-date

By the time the implementation stage has been reached, all major decisions concerning the recovery solution have been made and the scope of the implementation project should have been defined.

The project to implement the recovery solution will cover three main areas:

- Setting up the alternate recovery facility
- Developing and implementing the technical procedures to support the recovery solution
- Developing the recovery plan

The overall implementation project could also be divided into several sub-projects, which could then be assigned to individuals or teams to implement. The number of sub-projects will depend on the size and complexity of your DP installation.

Set Up the Alternate Recovery Facility

The decision regarding the type of recovery site should have already been made (see "Select the Recovery Site" on page 106). Detailed specifications for the recovery site and the facilities it will house also need to be defined. The implementation tasks that need to be completed vary, depending on the type of alternate site solution that has been selected. You may need to build and equip a new recovery facility, acquire or refit an existing site, or negotiate and sign a contract with a third party service provider.

Setting up a company-owned second site entails a major project in its own right and this is not addressed in detail here. If the recovery solution includes contracting to a commercial hot site, the following considerations should be taken into account:

- Length or duration of contract versus costs
- Distance from primary site
- Ease of upgrading when required
- Test time included in contract

- Size and technology used at the site (Can it accommodate your growth?)
- Cancellation clauses in the contract
- Number of subscribers allowed within a specified area or building
- Support services
- If cold site is included in contract
- Network capabilities
- Physical security

Develop Disaster Recovery Procedures

New procedures have to be created and existing procedures have to be amended to ensure that the critical business processes can be recovered and run at the recovery site. Some examples of the types of procedures that need to be developed or modified are:

- Data backup procedures

  Although most organizations currently back up data, many have not done an in-depth study to determine when certain data should be backed up, how it should be backed up, and how many generations should be kept off-site. Therefore, once the business impact analysis has been done, the changes need to be reflected in the existing (or new) data backup procedures for each application.

  It may be necessary to have a set of backups for disaster recovery separate from production backups because of the cycling rules. For instance, for production you may want to have the most current generation on-site, but for disaster recovery you will want the most current generation off-site. For this purpose it may be worthwhile to establish a backup file naming convention for disaster recovery (DR).

- Off-site storage procedures

Once the backup requirements of the data have been determined, procedures must be developed to implement the new cycling rules into the tape management system and to ensure that all new DR backups are cycled off-site. Some of the data that needs to be kept off-site, but not necessarily cycled, will be in hardcopy format. This could be special forms, documentation, or reference guides that will be needed for the recovery or to perform a job function once the system is up and running at the alternate facility. Refer to section "Documentation" on page 138 later in this chapter. The off-site procedures should provide an auditing capability to ensure critical data and documentation are being kept or cycled off-site on a regular basis.

If your solution includes electronic transfer of data to the alternate facility, you must provide procedures for the management and security of this data.

- Data recovery procedures

  It will also be necessary to develop or amend recovery procedures to restore all critical data at the recovery center. These data recovery procedures need to reflect the new data backup and off-site storage procedures.

- Change management procedures

  Change management usually pertains to changes in the current production DP environment. It is usually conducted through online change request forms and weekly reviews for approval of the requested changes. A section pertaining to impact on disaster recovery must be added to all of the current change management requests by the various departments. This will prevent the implementation changes that could have a severe impact on the recovery capability without anyone's realizing it. Once the impact is known, the proper steps can be taken to ensure that the recovery viability is not compromised.

- Application design rules

  The best time to evaluate an application's critical importance and impact to DR is at the design and development stages. This allows one to create applications that are easily recoverable and to react to the changes that may be necessary, such as contracting or acquiring additional disk or processor capacity at the alternate facility. Rules should therefore be put in place to ensure that recovery requirements are determined during design and development and have been implemented prior to moving the new application from development into production.

- Human resources procedures

  Steps should be taken at this time to draft company policies or procedures that will address the *human resources* issues that arise in a disaster situation. Such policies and procedures may address how employees are notified of a disaster, who works and who does not, compensation, counselling, and the recovery progress.

Develop the Recovery Plan

A disaster recovery plan is a comprehensive, detailed document stating all of the actions to be taken before, during, and after a disaster occurs.

Generally speaking, once the recovery solution has been implemented and the plan has been developed, the "before" steps refer to the maintenance of the plan, the "during" steps refer to the execution of the plan at time of disaster, and the "after" steps refer to the preparation for the return to the home site.

The development of a comprehensive, viable disaster recovery plan for a large system can only be accomplished as part of a major implementation project. Although some automation is possible, disaster recovery is basically a manual task. The preparedness and skill of the people involved can have a significant effect on the speed and success of the recovery.

Plan Contents

The recovery plan should include such things as:
- Recovery scope and assumptions
- The process for recognizing a disaster and invoking the plan
- Identification of the recovery teams and their members
- The major tasks and responsibilities of the recovery teams
- The owner of the plan
- How the plan will be maintained
- How the plan will be tested

As is the case in any large project, it is extremely important that everyone involved in the project understands the scope of the work to be done. The scope, assumptions, and general guidelines should have already been defined and clearly documented in the recovery plan.

Recognize the Disaster

A disaster does not necessarily cause immediate failure of the whole data center. Rather, it might start off as a series of gradual failures or as a seemingly limited damage. It is not always clear that a disaster has occurred. Also, the problem might happen at the worst possible time, during week-end or night shift, when experts are not readily available to assess the dimension of the problem. Such a situation is characterized by uncertainty and often confusion. Due to this confusion, procedures must be implemented that clearly define the action to be taken.

Most DP departments already use some form of operator procedure to document problem scenarios. As part of the disaster recovery strategy, this documentation must be extended to include guidelines on when a specific problem should be declared a disaster and what steps to take to escalate the issue. Such documentation may not cover every possible situation in detail, but in most cases it will allow a more objective and accurate assessment of the situation.

The scope of these scenarios may range from containable problems such as a link failure on an important network connection, or a data check on a database, to really extreme situations such as a fire in the machine room or total destruction by an earthquake. The former problems can usually be recovered in-house, while the latter problems are obviously the domain of disaster recovery.

These problems require different problem determination steps, action plans, and escalation procedures as well as different people to resolve them. The escalation procedures and escalation times depend on the structure of the DP organization and on the importance of the failing components.

At certain times, it will be necessary to involve someone with the skills to determine if and when disaster recovery should be initiated. We call this person the *disaster recovery coordinator*. This role is described in detail in "Disaster Recovery Coordinator" on page 126.

At what point is the Disaster Recovery Coordinator notified that things are out of line? As already noted, disasters do tend to creep up; they often arise from a series of apparently unrelated events. A possible criterion for notifying the Disaster Recovery Coordinator is any event or problem that the DP manager cannot solve through the normal problem management process.

Invoke the Disaster Recovery Plan

Making the decision and starting the move to an alternate site usually involves considerable expense for the company. This decision is not to be taken lightly. The decision should be made only by senior management who fully understand the effect the move might have on the organization.

Further, this decision will normally not be made quickly. It may be some time before enough information is available to actually make the decision.

Information Policy

An event as serious as a disaster will most certainly attract publicity both internally and externally.

Some companies or departments maintain rigorous guidelines in their information policy covering exactly what information can be disseminated to whom and when it can be disseminated. Some organizations create the messages in advance so that the information can be strictly controlled. Special care is often exercised with press releases. The need for this strict control will differ depending on the type of organization and the scope of the disaster.

The considerations in this area include:

• Who may inform external, official organizations?

- Which organizations do you want to inform?
- How detailed may the information be?
- What information may be distributed? What may not?
  - Reason for the disaster or outage
  - Effect and impact of the disaster
  - Whether there were injuries or deaths
  - Kind and amount of the damage to property
  - Expected duration of outage
  - Actions and progress
  - Impact to the company
  - Guilty persons
- What method of distribution is to be used?
  - Electronic mailing
  - Phone call
  - Telefax
  - Written message
  - Press release

Shift Schedule

The aim of disaster recovery is to re-establish processing as quickly as possible. Therefore, all those involved in the recovery will work under extreme stress and pressure. After twelve or more hours, the ability to concentrate and to work reliably will decrease. Even in a disaster situation, everybody needs sleep and relaxation. This must be considered when planning the schedules, responsibilities, and backups for the employees.

In some cases, there may be the need to impose certain restrictions on your customers and users. Limitations might involve:

- Network capacity and performance
- Numbers of connected terminals and workstations

- Online and service windows

Business Interfaces

The move to an alternate site will mean a change in telephone numbers and delivery addresses. Suppliers, couriers, common carriers, and other partners must be made aware of the new situation. It is useful to consider automatic redirection agreements with any suppliers.

Many DP environments require provisions for print output post-processing, such as paper separation, mass mailing, and so on. These facilities will also be required at the recovery site. If there is a significant distance between your prime and alternate site, delivery times of print output may be restricted. You may also need to establish new courier services to distribute the printed lists.

Return to Primary Site

The disaster recovery plan should include a section covering the return to the primary site. Many of the tasks are similar to the move to the alternate site, although in this case the move will be planned and more controlled. The level of effort and detail applied to planning this activity in advance of a disaster will depend on how long you can and will stay at the alternate site. Given enough time at the alternate site, the plan to return to the primary site could be developed after the disaster.

If the alternate site happens to be a commercial hot site, you may be able to stay there for up to six weeks only. In this case, you may need to plan for an interim move to a cold site facility as well as the final return to your primary site.

Disaster Recovery Teams and Key Roles

The recovery solution will be implemented through a series of major tasks assigned to the various recovery teams and key individuals. Each of the major tasks will consist of multiple sub-tasks which can be assigned to individual members of each team as knowledge or expertise dictates.

The tasks and responsibilities of these teams will differ based upon the disaster recovery strategy chosen and the organizational structure involved. Also, depending on the scope of the disaster and the amount of work in the recovery process, some people might participate full-time and others might participate part-time. In some cases, teams that are required during the preparation project may not be required as part of the ongoing maintenance or execution of the recovery. (An example of this would be the teams responsible for building and equipping a second site.)

In a large system data center, several recovery teams will be required. In a smaller data center such as a mid-range AS/400, only two or three teams may be needed. As stated earlier, management always plays a key role in disaster recovery and therefore there will always be a "management" team in addition to the teams from the operational and technical areas. There should never be fewer than two teams, and all team members should have an alternate who can fill in for them if they are unavailable at the time of disaster.

The recovery teams will be established according to the complexity of the recovery solution and they will have four primary responsibilities:

1. Write the recovery plan project tasks as requested.

2. Develop and implement the procedures needed in the production environment to support the recovery plan.

3. Execute the recovery steps as documented in the recovery plan during testing or disaster.

4. Maintain the procedures and recovery documentation pertinent to their areas.

The following is a list and description of key individuals and teams that may be involved in the development and execution of the disaster recovery plan.

Project Leader

The role of the project leader is to assume the overall responsibility for the project. This person supports the Disaster Recovery Coordinator in controlling and coordinating the tasks and facilitating communication between management, teams, and users. The project leader must ensure that the project is on schedule and is fulfilling the intent of the recovery solution.

Disaster Recovery Coordinator

The Disaster Recovery Coordinator (DRC) usually manages the problem situation and, at some point, informs senior management that a decision to move might be needed. After this decision, the Disaster Recovery Coordinator manages all teams that are involved in moving the computer center workload to the alternate site. The DRC takes responsibility for coordinating and controlling all tasks, problems, and procedures during disaster recovery.

The Disaster Recovery Coordinator needs to be sufficiently skilled in DP to accomplish the these tasks. Just as important is the ability to manage a complex project and people under stress. A Disaster Recovery Coordinator's attributes should include:

- Superior organizational skills
- Working technical knowledge of all areas involved
- Excellent interpersonal skills
- Good understanding of organizational structure and responsibilities
- Good understanding of the organization's business requirements

The DRC's responsibilities are divided between the implementation of the recovery solution and the ongoing maintenance of the recovery solution. During the implementation stage, the DRC acts as the liaison between the recovery teams and the project leader. In some cases, the DRC and the project leader may be the same person.

The DRC is responsible for reviewing the task deliverables, which are:

- Interfacing between the prime site and the alternate recovery site
- Arranging the staffing of the recovery test during the implementation phase

The DRC's ongoing responsibilities include:

- Acting as a buffer between prime site and recovery site
- Interfacing with change management
- Incorporating changes into plan document
- Coordinating plan testing
- Interfacing with management regarding disaster recovery status

The project will require approximately 75% of the DRC's time. Upon completion, ongoing responsibilities will require 25% of the DRC's time.

Disaster Recovery Steering Committee

The Steering Committee is usually headed by either the CEO, Managing Director, or General Manager of an organization and includes senior managers from areas such as DP, Finance, Administration, and Human Resources. This committee will ultimately decide whether to declare a disaster or not, based on input from the DRC and technical/operational specialists. In most cases, the members of this committee will already have been involved in the problem determination and escalation process for the outage.

They are generally responsible for:

- Disaster declaration
- Disaster notification
- Supporting DRC
- Making or executing recovery policies
- Providing senior management commitment
- Providing for publicity and media relations

Alternate Site Manager

The role of the Alternate Site Manager requires some clarification. This is usually the normal data center operations manager in a small business, or the operations supervisors in a large business open 24 hours every day. Although these individuals may have minimal responsibility during the implementation phase, they must be familiar with the disaster recovery policies and procedures. They are in charge of the recovery facility data center once the recovery has been completed.

Auditors

Auditors are important in disaster recovery. The proof of the viability of the recovery plan rests largely on the auditors' shoulders. In many organizations, there are both internal and external auditors. Consultants who specialize in disaster recovery planning could be hired to take the external auditor role. Auditors participate in the implementation and testing of the recovery solution to ensure it fulfills its obligations set by the senior management of the organization.

The internal audit department is responsible for ensuring the integrity and the security of the data restored at the alternate recovery facility as well as the integrity of the financial status of the business data. This entails detailed knowledge of the data reconciliation procedures executed at the recovery facility in order to recover the business data and transactions to current status. All transactions lost as a result of the disaster should be accounted for.

The internal audit department should be especially diligent in carrying out these functions during testing of the disaster recovery plan to ensure successful recovery in the event of an actual disaster.

Management Team

This team will consist of those individuals, other than or in addition to the Steering Committee, who are in a position to resolve issues concerning the policies, resources, finances, and other matters involved in completing the project or for ongoing costs. The corporate auditor should be a part of this team.

Administrative Team

This team will be responsible for setting up the control center to monitor the recovery process. This may be at the alternate site, another company location, or even a hotel. The administration team will arrange for supplies, office equipment, telephones, and PCs that may be required. The control center will be used by management to monitor the progress at the alternate site and to carry on high level management functions. In addition, this team should help with the logging of logistical problems encountered during the recovery. These logs will be extremely useful in future refinements of the disaster recovery plan. The help desk personnel will also work from the control center if the primary site has been destroyed or is inaccessible.

Information and Help Desk Team

In a disaster situation it is vital to distribute the right information at the right time to the right people. This is discussed further in "Information Policy" on page 122. This team should have a list of what people and organizations, internal and external, must be informed and what information they should receive. Preparing this list in advance will ensure that no time is lost in initiating this communication and that no one is overlooked. Once all parties are notified, the information team may assume help desk functions.

Hardware and Installation Team

A hardware and installation team is needed when your recovery strategy requires the purchase and installation of additional hardware. All capacity and installation aspects should be planned and prepared in advance, and the steps and tasks of this team should be clearly documented.

Off-site Storage Team

All recovery strategies will include the transfer of backup tapes from an off-site facility to the recovery site unless data mirroring or electronic vaulting is being done for all data. This team will be responsible for the off-site cycling of the tapes or documents at the prime site under normal production circumstances as well as for the retrieval of the off-site tapes during testing and in the case of an actual disaster. All tasks of the off-site storage team should be defined and described in the disaster recovery plan, for example:

- Directions to the off-site facility
- Access to the off-site facility
- How to identify daily, weekly, monthly, or incremental backup tapes and their generations
- Packing and transport of the tapes to the recovery site

Network Team

For cost or availability reasons, an organization may choose not to fully configure the backup network in advance. In this case, there will be some configuration work to be done as part of the recovery.

This work may include the purchase, installation, and customization of additional modems or lines. As part of disaster recovery planning, confirm that the required number of modems or lines will be available for purchase or installation in the event of a disaster.

Depending on your network layout and solution, activities such as line switching or customizing controllers in remote locations may be necessary. For these tasks, you need predefined network capacity and layout plans including procedures describing where and how the tasks are to be performed. Some examples of network recovery steps are:

- Switching of lines at the alternate site
- Maintaining external network controllers
- Assigning ports
- Producing schematic of network for alternate site
- Providing maintenance and documentation for these recovery steps

Software Team

The software recovery team is involved in the recovery of the required systems and applications to the alternate site. In a large DP environment, you may choose to have separate software teams for the operating system, the database, network, and so on. In a smaller shop, one software team may encompass all of these areas. Generally speaking, this team is responsible for restoring the DP platforms, catalogues, and applications with the latest backups available. The tasks and responsibilities of these teams are too extensive to cover in this section and are discussed in *Disaster Recovery Library S/390 Technology Guide* (see "International Technical Support Organization Publications" on page 193). However, here are some examples:

- Identifying critical system software required at the alternate site
- Preparing strategy of the restore process
- Performing system restore procedures
- Performing system checkout procedures
- Documenting system software

Operations Team

The Operations Team is usually the team that executes the steps for recovery as documented in the Disaster Recovery Plan. This team provides resources to man the consoles and looks after print and tape requirements. Once the recovery has been accomplished, it assumes the ongoing running of the alternate site data center. Some responsibilities it may have to support disaster recovery are:

- Establishing length and staffing of shifts during recovery
- Modifying procedures for batch submission as required
- Modifying job setup and scheduling procedures
- System checkout procedures
- Amending initiator structure

Application Support Team

This team should consist of the people, such as programmers and developers, who are responsible for the applications that support the critical business processes. Members of this team may be called upon to develop new programs or processes to aid in the smooth recovery of the business processes at time of disaster. The Application Support Team will work closely with the Business Units during the development of the recovery plan. Some additional responsibilities it may have to support disaster recovery are:

- Determining the test strategy for the applications
- Developing the application recovery procedures
- Performing checkout of applications after recovery

Business Users Team

The business users are the individuals in the various Business Units who use the applications to perform the organization's business processes. Members of this team are generally responsible for ensuring that the business process has been recovered successfully and that all critical functions within the processes can be performed. Their recovery responsibilities include:

- Developing business process procedures for the alternate site
- Documenting data reconciliation procedures

- Developing checkout procedures for the business processes
- Identifying business material required for off-site
- Developing manual procedures if required

The number, structure, and size of the recovery teams will vary with every organization. The important thing to remember is that no team members should be required to perform multiple recovery functions at the same time; therefore, team members should only be on one team to avoid conflict.

In addition to the team responsibilities previously listed, all teams are responsible for the ongoing maintenance and testing of the recovery procedures as set out in the "maintenance" section of the plan document. Plan maintenance is discussed further in the next chapter.

Example Plan

Table 1 shows the elements of a typical recovery plan. The details of the plan will be different for each organization.

Table 1 (Page 1 of 2). *Example of Recovery Plan Elements*

Part	Function	Contents
Plan Overview	General information about the document and recovery responsibilities	Purpose and scope Initiating disaster recovery activities Recovery structure Recovery team responsibilities
Recovery Procedures	Procedures to execute the recovery at the alternate site	Off-site data recovery procedures System restore procedures Operations procedures Network recovery procedures Application recovery procedures
Plan Testing	Procedures to test the viability of the recovery plan	System testing procedures Applications testing procedures Testing strategies Test reporting
Plan Administration	Description of all processes and procedures to maintain the plan	Plan change control Plan distribution Plan auditing Team maintenance responsibilities

Table 1 (Page 2 of 2). *Example of Recovery Plan Elements*

Part	Function	Contents
Return to Primary Site	High level steps to provide for the return to the primary site	Access to primary site building Backup strategy Recovery strategy Relinquishing the recovery site Physical security
Appendix	Lists, reference documentation, hardware and disk configurations and so on, supporting the tasks, processes and procedures in the preceding chapters	Names, addresses, and phone numbers of disaster recovery participants; internal and external personnel Normal and backup configurations of system and network Inventory of critical applications, files and databases Service level agreements Message to newspapers, TV Signatures

Confidentiality and Access to the Plan

As the recovery plan contains strategic company policy and technical information, most companies declare the plan confidential and keep all copies secure. Thus, you should keep the number of recipients to a minimum. Only the members of the disaster recovery teams (including auditors) should possess a copy of the plan.

Make sure that at least one copy of your plan is kept at the alternate facility or another off-site location that is accessible at all times. You should also make sure that the team leaders of each team have "home" and "office" copies of the plan.

Plan Development Tools

In a large and complex DP environment, it may be useful to purchase a "plan development tool" to assist with the gathering and input of information, as well as the structure of the plan. There are many such tools in the market place, but most of them will require training and in some cases it may take several weeks to become comfortable with a tool. The organization should assess the value a planning tool will provide versus the use of a word processing tool that is currently installed and known by the individuals responsible for the development and maintenance of the recovery plan.

Plan Ownership and Maintenance

The DRC is usually the owner of the recovery plan and is responsible for the administration of its maintenance. Most sections are maintained by recovery teams, although the DRC may maintain some sections. The following chapter will discuss plan maintenance and testing in more detail.

Documentation

In addition to developing and documenting a disaster recovery plan, other DP documentation will also need to be reviewed, enhanced, and reorganized. There are three categories of documentation that must be considered:

- Official manuals and publications about hardware, software, products, concepts, and solutions
- Standards and procedures for daily operations
- Specific disaster recovery documentation

The main consideration for the first category is to ensure that the manuals required at the alternate site are available. The following discussion will focus on the other two categories of documentation, that is, the daily procedures and the disaster recovery documents.

A regular transfer of all required documentation to the recovery site or some other safe site is essential. Also, make sure that the latest versions of all the documents are electronically available, even in the event of a disaster.

Existing Documents

As part of the daily operation of the DP organization, there are various documents that assist in the management of the DP facilities, environments, network, host and peripheral equipment, services, applications, and data.

The implementation of a disaster recovery strategy increases the complexity and dependencies of the DP processes. As a result, there are changes in procedures and standards, and these must be reflected in the existing documentation. The following are examples of likely areas of change:

- Systems and network management
- Configuration management, resource and capacity planning
- Change management
- Problem management
- Operations processes and procedures
- Data backup concept and procedures
- Application programming standards
- Security

New Documents

The implementation of an alternate site for disaster recovery may also involve the creation of a number of new documents, such as:

- Disaster Recovery Strategy

  The strategy document refers to the overall description of a disaster recovery solution and contains the overall characteristics and major components of the target solution. The section entitled "Design the Backup/Recovery Solution" on page 43 lists the elements that a strategy document should contain.

The document may also contain information about residual risks, the current status of the strategy implementation, and any open problems that might have arisen during the last recovery test.

- Recovery Test

  A document about recovery testing helps the disaster recovery or test coordinator to plan, execute, and review recovery tests. It should contain:

  - Information about test frequency
  - Checklists for test preparation
  - Forms to record test results
  - Schedule plans and test processes
  - Summaries of the test results
  - Checklists for the review of the results and the implementation of improvements

  These items are described in more detail in "Test the Plan" on page 150.

- Service Level Agreements

  Service level agreements describe the services and performance levels that will be delivered by DP to the various users. "Service Level Agreements for DR" on page 37 describes the components of the service level agreements.

The key thing to remember about disaster recovery documentation is that information that is already contained in other manuals, files, and other publications should only be referenced in the actual disaster recovery plan, not duplicated. This will cut down the maintenance time and keep the recovery plan focused on the actual steps that need to be executed to recover in a timely manner.

You must ensure that all referenced documents will be available in a disaster.

Keep the Solution Up-to-Date

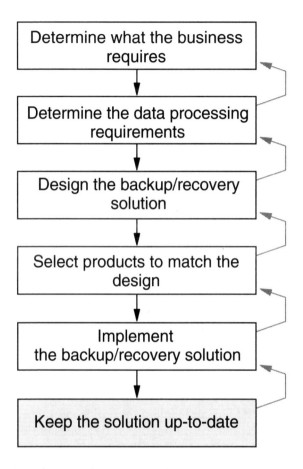

Once the disaster recovery plan has been developed and the recovery solution has been implemented, procedures to keep the recovery solution viable must be put in effect before the project is closed. Changes to the DP environment in a large datacenter are constant, and any change could render the recovery plan unusable.

These procedures should incorporate these three distinct elements, namely:

1. Maintenance
2. Auditing
3. Testing

Maintenance

The purpose of "maintenance" procedures is to provide a mechanism for updating the recovery solution when changes are made to the environment that may impact the plan's viability, to provide for ongoing testing of the plan, and to provide for ongoing training of staff.

Changes that may affect the recovery solution can come from many sources, such as:

- Development of new applications
- Changes to current hardware configuration
- Changes to the network
- Organizational changes
- System changes
- Changes to the alternate site

Change Management

Most DP installations will already have a formal process for managing and controlling changes to their environment. The Disaster Recovery Coordinator (DRC) must be a part of the change management process to evaluate the impact of upcoming changes on the recovery solution and to identify all corequisite changes (to the solution itself, to the plan and to the procedures) that must also be implemented.

There should be an integrated change management system for the entire organization, to provide a single point of control. All planned changes must be reviewed for their impact on the disaster recovery plan because any change may affect the viability of the plan. For example, a simple configuration change may have a significant impact on the alternate site. The decision to make a change may need to be reconsidered if the impact is too great. This is especially true if the alternate site is a company-owned second site. Of course, if a change is made at the prime site, it may not be necessary or appropriate to make the identical change at the second site (or in some cases, to make any change at all). These factors must all be assessed by the change management function.

As with changes to the prime site, all changes to the disaster recovery site must be identified to the DRC for evaluation and impact to the plan. The Disaster Recovery Coordinator should be a member of the change management committee to ensure that all proposed changes are consistent with the disaster recovery plan.

While running in disaster mode at the recovery center, a "change freeze" should be enforced until the business processes are fully operational and stable. Only emergency changes to bypass or fix severe problems should be allowed.

Some of the major types of changes that can have an effect on the disaster recovery plan are discussed in the following section.

Hardware Configuration Changes

When changes are made to the hardware environment at the prime site, be sure to determine what impact these changes will have on the disaster recovery plan and manage the changes accordingly. Changes in this area could impact the performance objectives. For example, if the real or expanded storage of the prime site processor is increased, the performance of an application will be different when executed at the recovery site. Similarly, if the configuration of channels or disk devices changes at one site, there will be a performance or capacity impact at the other site.

Application Changes

It is essential that if applications or application programs are developed or modified in any way at the prime site, those changes are applied to the recovery solution as well. The change management team must determine the most appropriate manner in which to ensure that the "impact at time of disaster" has been assessed and provided for prior to the application's or program's being accepted into the production environment.

New applications must be assessed for their critical value and whether new disaster recovery procedures are required. When disaster recovery is required, change management must ensure the procedures are in place and notify capacity planning of the new workload for disaster recovery. Products such as SUNRISE* should be used on a regular basis to ensure that all data sets and programs required by the critical applications are being sent off-site and are included in the restore process.

Software Environment Changes

If your alternate site is a company-owned second site, it is important to consider the impact of the operating system environment's at the second site not being identical to that of the primary site. Ideally, the operating system environment at both sites should be identical, though in reality this is not always possible. When planning your disaster recovery site, make sure that the advantages and disadvantages of identical or mirrored systems are considered. *Disaster Recovery Library S/390 Technology Guide*, GG24-4210 (see "International Technical Support Organization Publications" on page 193) describes in detail the considerations in this respect.

If your alternate site is a commercial hot site, you must ensure that all major changes to the operating system, such as a new release of MVS or JES, have been tested at the alternate site as part of the testing strategy. These types of changes should be done as a test on their own and not as part of a full test. Problems encountered during the restore of the operating platform will usually prevent any applications testing from taking place due to time constraints. It is important that you contact your software vendors for instructions on the licensing of their products on a processor at the alternate site at time of disaster. Processor-dependent software, along with the vendor's name and contact number, should be clearly documented in the disaster recovery plan.

Update the Plan

Documented procedures must be developed by the Disaster Recovery Coordinator to ensure that the maintenance practices put in place are adequate to sustain the viability of the plan at all times.

The maintenance section of the recovery plan should clearly indicate the scope of responsibility that each team or key individual has for maintenance purposes. All areas of the recovery solution must be covered. No team should be responsible for the maintenance of information outside of their normal production responsibilities (with the possible exception of the DRC).

It is recommended that revisions be handled on a monthly or bi-monthly basis. If the revision process is kept on a regular cycle, the teams will know when changes are due and are more likely to perform regular reviews of their areas of responsibility. The DRC should make sure that all teams or key individuals respond to the plan revision process even if no changes have occurred in their area of responsibility. In this way, the DRC will know that even though there were no changes, the documentation was reviewed.

A "revision control form" should be created and included as part of the recovery plan maintenance procedures. This form should provide a place for the following:

- The originating team or department
- Type of change (new or modification)
- Which section of the plan the change applies to
- Required signatures

A cross check of the *plan distribution* should be done against the *revision control forms* handed in each update month to ensure all plan holders have submitted the form. A maintenance report should then be issued to the plan holders and management showing the status (that is, complete or incomplete).

Audit the Plan

The only sure way to determine if updates or changes to the disaster recovery plan document have taken place is to audit them. Plan contents should be audited on a semi-annual or annual basis taking the following into account:

- Documents should not all be taken for audit at the same time.
- All audited documents should be returned to the holder within 24 hours.
- All home copies of the documents should not be audited at the same time.
- Documents should be audited against the DRC's copy.
- Deficiencies should be noted and corrected before returning the document to the holder.
- A report should be issued to management documenting the status of each plan holder's document (that is, complete or incomplete).

In addition to auditing the contents of the DR plans, all major components of the recovery process should be audited on a monthly or bi-monthly basis. Examples of such components are:

- The critical file tape list to ensure that all required backup tapes are off-site

- The "onepack" or "emergency" system to ensure it is up-to-date. This system should also be tested occasionally at the prime site to make certain that it can be IPLed.

Test the Plan

An essential part of disaster recovery planning is testing or rehearsal. All too frequently, just creating a disaster recovery plan results in a false sense of security. Without testing, it is almost inevitable that the disaster recovery plan will just not work when a disaster occurs. Testing is also the only way to tell if your maintenance procedures are working. Once the plan has been developed and tested, the only way it can fail (barring destruction of the alternate site or off-site storage facility) is if maintenance has not been correctly performed.

Whenever possible, you should choose a remote site recovery strategy that allows you to test frequently. Testing your disaster recovery tasks and procedures has the following benefits:

- Knowledge that the recovery plan works
- Discovery of problems, mistakes, and errors which can then be resolved
- Training of employees in executing tests and managing disaster recovery situations
- Making the recovery plan a "living" document
- Raising awareness in all parts of the DP organization regarding the necessity of disaster recovery planning

There are two *types* of testing that should be performed. "Active" testing involves going to the alternate site and restoring the systems and applications as set out in the disaster recovery plan.

The other, "passive" test is a logistical test of the plan. It is generally conducted by gathering the recovery teams (including management) into a conference room and going through the steps each would do in the event of a disaster.

The steps covered would include problem escalation, disaster declaration procedures, assembling the teams, and so on. In this way, the management team can become familiar with the steps they will be responsible for and can make sure they can be accomplished as documented. (For example, if the documentation states that the DRC must contact the team members, and the disaster happens at midnight, then does the DRC have a means of obtaining the necessary phone numbers from home?)

Frequency of the Tests

Almost invariably, installations encounter a mini-disaster when they first test the disaster recovery plan; hopefully this is during the development stage. It is only through multiple attempts to recover that the flaws in the plan are highlighted.

It is therefore wise to plan on a number of tests during the development of the plan. Once plan development has been completed, tests should be carried out two to four times a year. The frequency will depend on:

- The interval between major changes in the hardware and software environment
- How current the recovery plan is to be kept
- How critical and sensitive the business processes are (the more critical they are, the more frequently testing may be required)

Under normal conditions, we suggest that the recovery plan be tested at least twice a year.

There are basically two approaches to testing: announced and unannounced.

In the announced rehearsal or test, the people involved know what is going to transpire. This is essentially a check that the procedures for recovery of the platform, data, and business processes are complete and accurate.

In the unannounced test, someone (with the agreement of senior management) "pulls the plug." The installation staff is informed that their data center is no longer operable and they must invoke the recovery plan.

Note: This is an extreme measure and can be very, very costly. It would be unwise to attempt it until a number of announced rehearsals have been successfully carried out.

Even organizations with a well-tested plan usually hesitate to attempt an unannounced rehearsal because there is a danger that normal operations will be severely impacted.

Test Levels

Each of the tests that are conducted at the alternate site will not be "full" tests of the disaster recovery plan. There are a number of levels of testing that should be considered as follows:

- Testing of the system platforms.

  Whenever there is a major change to the operating system, you should plan a mini-test at the alternate site to ensure that the operating system can be recovered and IPLed with the new software. You may wish to do limited network testing at this time as well.

- Testing of the network.

  Major changes to the network environment may require stand alone testing to verify that the connections can be established and data can be transmitted prior to executing a "full" test. The operating system will need to be restored as part of this process, along with some test data and test locations.

- Testing of the platforms, network, and selected applications and business processes.

  This is often referred to as a "full" test because it includes testing of all of the major components of recovery (such as system software, network, application, and business users) even though all applications or business processes may not be included in the test.

  Because of the disruption to personnel at the primary site, it is unusual to test all of the business processes in one test. Usually different processes are tested during each test so that all processes are tested sometime during the year. In a smaller organization, it may be possible to test all critical applications and business processes at the same time.

- Total transfer of service to the disaster recovery data center.

  Until this option has been exercised, you can't be absolutely certain that the disaster recovery plan will work effectively in an actual disaster.

  Nevertheless, it takes a great deal of courage to exercise this option. It is a very costly exercise, because it contains the very real risk that if the plan does not work, the fallback to the normal data center might well be impacted by failures during the rehearsal.

It would be impractical to attempt to recover all applications and business processes during the first application test. Each application or group of applications should be tested separately; then, when all of these have been recovered successfully, you can test the recovery of all applications together.

Activities before the Test

Planning for a major test should begin one to two months prior to the scheduled test date at the alternate site. If the alternate site is a commercial hot site, tests must be scheduled at least six weeks in advance. For large test slots (3 or 4 days), you may have to schedule your test slots a year in advance. If the alternate site is a company-owned second site, then enough notice must be provided to allow sufficient resources to be available for the test. The better the test preparation, the more efficient and successful the test will be.

Usually it is the responsibility of the Disaster Recovery Coordinator to prepare and coordinate the test. The following are some steps that should be included as part of the pre-test activities:

- Interface with the alternate site to ensure the test date has been scheduled and the resources are available.
- Each test should be preceded by a "walkthrough" with all participants.
- In general, the scheduled test should include the system, application, network, and business process components of the plan.

- A test schedule must be prepared and distributed to all team members prior to the test.
- Auditors should participate in all tests.
- Test objectives, criteria, approach, and activities should be documented and distributed to the team members.
- Staffing must be determined, including where individuals will be located. For example, you may have business staff at another company site or multiple company sites and technical staff at the alternate site.

The goals and deliverables for each function and process must be agreed to in advance to enable the measurement of the success achieved.

Acceptance Criteria

For each test, the acceptance criteria will vary depending on the objectives of the test. In general, the following must be achieved in each test:

- Systems software must provide a current version of the operating and application software systems with all major components enabled and functioning.
- At least one application must be recovered and tested, including application processing, batch, and data reconciliation. The exception to this would be a test of the operating system alone to test changes such as a new hardware configuration.
- All critical data must have come from the off-site storage facility.
- All deficiencies from the last test must be tested to ensure that they have been resolved.

Execute the Test

During the test, all procedures must be executed exactly as documented in the recovery plan unless some deviation has been agreed to. This requires that the plan is sufficiently detailed and complete and does not rely on the experience or knowledge of the participants.

Team members should execute only those parts of the plan that are within their scope of responsibility. As the test progresses, each member will note any required changes in their copy of the plan and log all problems and solutions (if any) in the problem log for review at the end of the test.

If a major problem is encountered, a meeting may be convened by the DRC to address the problem before proceeding with the test.

The alternate site should be staffed at all times during the test in case problems arise, so the scheduling of breaks, meals, day shifts, and night shifts is important. The schedule should ensure that no one works in excess of twelve consecutive hours during the test.

During the last few hours of the test slot or while "data cleanup" is taking place, the recovery team members should meet and document the events that transpired during the test while these events are still fresh in their memory.

After the Test

In the postmortem upon completion of the test, with the recovery team, the Disaster Recovery Coordinator prepares a test report. It states that the test has been conducted and indicates what deficiencies, if any, were encountered during the test. The test report should state the following:

- The objectives of the test and whether or not they were met.
- The problems encountered and who has been assigned to resolve them.
- Recommendations for improvement to the recovery process.
- A summary of the test.
- A report from internal audit stating their findings and impressions of the test.
- A report from the business units involved outlining the test results from a business perspective.

Depending on the severity of the problems, the test may be repeated immediately or the problem may be left to be resolved prior to the next test. Problems encountered during this test must be added to the objectives of the next test. Any changes required to the documentation as a result of the test must now be incorporated into the recovery plan. After the changes have been made, the revisions must be distributed to all plan holders.

Hints and Tips

Some circumstances may restrict the ability to test the disaster recovery concept. Some of these are:

- The network may need to run 24 hours a day, seven days a week. Therefore, testing the backup network might be very difficult or even impossible. In this case a temporary *test network* with its own paths and routes may have to be designed and configured.

- In another installation, the disk space for critical data may amount to hundreds of gigabytes. The restore time alone may render a full test impractical. In this case, the only option is to split the workload and test the different components separately.

- Interdependencies between applications can be a major hindrance. In some cases, testing may be impossible without redesigning some applications. A redesign may be acceptable if it is part of the chosen disaster recovery strategy. Otherwise, you may be able to test a simplified copy of these applications or test a group of applications that have interdependencies.

- Whenever your alternate site makes a change to its hardware configuration, make sure that you update the Disaster Recovery operating system accordingly.

- Testing your recovery plan mixed with an existing, running system on the second site might be very difficult and could affect daily production and processing on that system. Whenever possible, use LPARs with non-shared disks to test your disaster recovery environment.

Regular testing and maintenance practices will ensure that the disaster recovery plan keeps a high profile with the recovery staff and management.

Appendix A. System/390 Disaster Recovery Products

In general, the principles and steps in the development of a disaster recovery solution are similar whether you use a large mainframe or LAN connected PCs. In the body of this book we have discussed these steps generically so that they can be applied to any platform. In this appendix, however, we focus specifically on the System/390 (S/390) platform and review the main products and facilities that support faster and more effective disaster recovery.

The S/390 platform is a mature processing environment that provides many powerful products and facilities for backup and recovery. These products are briefly described here and covered in greater detail in *Disaster Recovery Library S/390 Technology Guide* (see "International Technical Support Organization Publications" on page 193).

Enterprise System Connection (ESCON)

In "Data Transport and Secure Storage" on page 62 and "Site Interconnection" on page 83, we discussed the option of placing disk and tape devices at the alternate site and channel connecting these devices to the primary. This configuration offers an efficient and simple way to transfer and maintain recovery data at the alternate site. For this option, you must have the ability to channel attach devices at suitable distances to satisfy your disaster recovery requirements; you also need the availability of sufficient bandwidth to sustain the data traffic to these devices.

Enterprise System Connection (ESCON) is an architecture that enables channel connection to devices and other processors at distances up to 60 km with a data transfer rate of 17 megabytes per second.

ESCON has greatly enhanced the interconnection capabilities between both processors and their I/O devices and between multiple processors. Processors and control units can be located on and interconnected between separate floors within a campus environment or separate on sites. Optical links are used for ESCON data transmission.

There are two implementations of ESCON. The first uses light emitting diode (LED) technology and can be used to extend the distance of I/O controllers and channel-to-channel connections to a maximum distance of 3km per link. Data is transferred at a rate of up to 9 megabytes per second.

The second implementation of ESCON is known as the Extended Data Feature (XDF) and utilizes laser technology. This allows the interconnection distances between processors and between processors and their attached I/O devices to be extended to 20km per link. Data is generally transferred at a rate of 17 megabytes per second.

The connection distances can be extended by combining multiple links using ESCON directors or repeaters.

Figure 24 on page 161 shows the interconnection capabilities using a combination of ESCON and ESCON XDF services. Note that most processors and devices do not support direct connection to ESCON XDF, so connection will almost always involve a combination of ESCON and ESCON XDF.

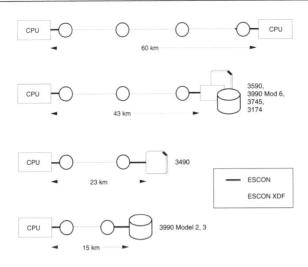

Figure 24. *System/390 ESCON Interconnection Options*

In Figure 24, ESCON directors or converters are used to connect multiple optical fiber links. A maximum of two ESCON directors and any number of repeaters can be used in any connection. However, there are limits to the distance that devices or processors can support at full performance. These distance limits are illustrated in Figure 24 and are as follows:

- 60 km for channel-to-channel (CTC) connections, that is, processor to processor connections
- 23 km from the CPU to 3990 Model 003 DASD controllers and 3490 cartridge tape controllers
- 43 km from the CPU to 3990 Model 006 DASD controllers and 3590 cartridge tape controllers

Exceeding these distance limits will result in reduced performance or, beyond a certain point, may not work at all. If you need to exceed these distance limits, IBM can analyze your individual situation and determine if your configuration will work and what performance degradations, if any, you will have to expect.

Using ESCON XDF channel connections, you can design configurations sufficient for many disaster recovery needs. Primary and secondary sites 60 km apart can now utilize high bandwidth CTC connections for the transfer of backup data. Channel connected DASD and cartridge drives can be located 43 km and 23 km, respectively, from the primary site, allowing copies of critical data to be transferred off-site simply and efficiently.

Traditional backup processes depend on the production of backup cartridges that are manually transported off-site. These cartridges often reside at the primary site for hours after they are produced because they are awaiting transport. With remotely connected DASD or cartridges, this data is safe immediately after the backup is complete. In addition, the highly manual process of cartridge management can be completely avoided.

If your enterprise has a large campus with multiple S/390 processor and device locations, you can build your own ESCON infrastructure as an ideal medium to interconnect these. If, however, there is public land between your computer locations, the service of a telecommunications company is required. Telecommunications companies in many countries now offer "dark fiber" links over public land that can be used for ESCON.

3990 Model 006 Remote Copy

Typically, the most time-consuming component of a recovery is restoring the data and bringing it up-to-date. "Readiness of the Alternate Site" on page 64 discusses the concept of data currency, or data readiness, at the alternate site. If a reasonably current copy of the critical data can be maintained at the alternate site, recovery time can be dramatically reduced and the potential to lose data updates in the disaster can be minimized.

The remote copy function of the 3990 Model 006 DASD Controller enables realtime copies of DASD volumes to be maintained at a remote site. Little or no data is lost in the disaster and recovery can consist of connecting this data to the recovery processor and restarting the system.

There are two distinct implementations of remote copy: peer-to-peer remote copy (PPRC) and extended remote copy (XRC). Both PPRC and XRC enable you to copy any type of data on a disk volume.

PPRC

The configuration for PPRC is illustrated in Figure 25. PPRC provides synchronous data copying capability from one 3990 Model 006 to another 3990 Model 006. This ensures full DASD data currency in the event of an outage at the primary site. Updates are sent from the primary 3990 Model 006 directly to the secondary 3990 Model 006 through ESCON links between the two 3990 Model 006s (the host is not involved in the primary to secondary transfer). The 3990 Model 006s can be up to 43 km (26.7 miles) apart.

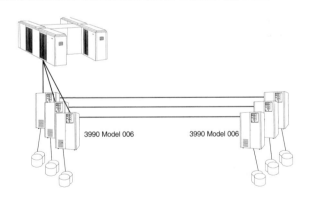

Figure 25. Peer-to-Peer Remote Copy

To ensure full data currency at the recovery site, the update is not considered complete by the application until the data is written to both 3990s. The unavoidable performance impact of this requirement is mitigated by the ability of the 3990s to consider a write as complete once the update is in the controller cache.

XRC

The configuration for XRC is illustrated in Figure 26 on page 165. XRC provides an asynchronous data copying capability with data on the secondary volume typically maintained a few seconds to a few minutes behind the data at the primary site.

This function is implemented through a combination of the 3990 Model 006 and DFSMS/MVS software. Updates to data are copied asynchronously by DFSMS/MVS from a 3990 Model 006 at the primary site to DASD at a recovery site.

The DFSMS/MVS system can be located at the primary site, at the secondary location, or in a separate system located elsewhere, but it must be connected to both the primary and secondary DASD controllers.

Primary and secondary DASD controllers can be attached to the DFSMS/MVS host up to 43 kilometers (26.7 miles) through ESCON links. Parallel channel attachment is also supported with XRC, but considerably limits the performance and distance.

Distance limitations are virtually eliminated in XRC environments that utilize channel extenders such as the CHANNELink* systems offered by Computer Network Technology (CNT) Corporation. This capability is also useful in cases where an ESCON service is not publicly available.

The performance impact of XRC is typically greatly reduced as compared to PPRC in the same environments, due to the asynchronous design of XRC.

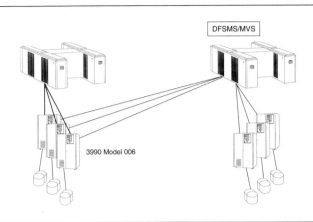

Figure 26. *Extended Remote Copy*

For disaster recovery, remote copy offers some significant benefits. First, changes made at the primary site are transported real-time to the alternate site. This means that in the event of a disaster, minimal data is lost. In the case of PPRC, this data loss is zero. Any updates completed at the primary site will have been reflected at the alternate site. For XRC, assuming adequate capacity, the data loss will be small, typically minutes or seconds, which is an enormous improvement on the potential losses from more traditional backup methods.

Second, the data copying is system-managed; the hardware and software involved ensure that data changes at the primary site are correctly duplicated at the alternate site. This avoids the requirement for complex backup and restore procedures to recover and synchronize the data.

Finally, recovery is greatly simplified, resulting in a reduced recovery time and fewer potential errors. Following a disaster, the copied data can be made available through a single recovery command.

The choice of implementation, PPRC or XRC, depends on the recovery requirements. PPRC should be used when no data loss can be tolerated and the performance impact on the application system is acceptable. PPRC can be used only when the two sites are within 43 km of each other. When longer distances are required or when application performance is critical, XRC should be considered.

CMOS Processors (IBM 9672)

One of the largest costs in disaster recovery is the cost of the alternate site's hardware and facilities. The use of a disaster recovery service reduces this cost, but the cost usually remains significant. As discussed in "Decision Criteria" on page 98, your final disaster recovery solution is always a trade-off between the ideal solution and an acceptable cost. CMOS processors reduce the cost of processing hardware and the required facilities and therefore allow you to consider recovery options that may be otherwise too expensive. They also introduce new options for the "housing" of the processor capacity.

CMOS stands for Complementary Metal Oxide Semiconductor. It is the microprocessor technology used by IBM in all of the most recently-developed processors. CMOS technology is not new, but until recently it could not support the necessary performance requirements of large processors.

The use of CMOS provides cost benefits in two major areas. First, CMOS technology is less expensive to manufacture than the bipolar technology that was previously used for large systems. This is in part because CMOS technology is used in many products, from large processors down to PCs. Second, CMOS-based processors enable significant environmental savings. The previous generation of large processors (based on bipolar technology) were water cooled, which required specialized cooling equipment. They used more power and space and were more expensive to maintain. When migrating from a bipolar machine to a CMOS machine, there may be reductions of up to 85% in energy costs (including power and air-conditioning), up to 65% in service and maintenance costs, and more than a 86% reduction in the floor space taken by the machine.

The move to CMOS-based processing has a number of implications for disaster recovery. Disaster recovery typically requires the existence of some amount of redundant processing capacity. Even if the alternate site is owned by you, it is difficult to balance the workload in such a way as to successfully utilize all processing resources at both sites. As CMOS makes this redundant equipment less expensive, disaster recovery becomes more affordable.

CMOS also opens up new options in alternate site facilities. The fact that CMOS processors are smaller, require no water cooling, and require lower levels of power and air conditioning means that a specialized computer room may no longer be needed. Using office space or even a mobile service for recovery becomes possible.

Parallel Sysplex

In "Workload Distribution across Two Sites" on page 90, we discuss the difficulties of balancing workload evenly across the primary and alternate sites. The same principle holds even for a single site with multiple processors. In the ideal world, this balancing would be automatic and workload would run wherever it could find the resources, even across sites. In addition, the failure of any single component (a processor, a DASD volume or a controller) would be automatically handled by switching to another equivalent resource.

The S/390 Parallel Sysplex offers this ideal world completely within a single site and partially across multiple sites.

A Parallel Sysplex consists of multiple systems coupled by hardware and software services. Parallel Sysplex uses high performance data sharing with new coupling technology to couple together multiple MVS/ESA systems to provide continuous availability,

When a processor in the Parallel Sysplex fails, its workload can be automatically shifted to another processor in the Parallel Sysplex.

A Parallel Sysplex has the following elements:

- Inter-system communication, which makes it possible to signal the presence or absence of systems or applications in a multi-system environment. The cross-system coupling facility (XCF) is the inter-system communication manager in a sysplex.

- A common time reference called the Sysplex Timer, which allows events on different systems to be handled in the proper sequence. The Timer provides a common time reference for systems monitoring and problem determination in a sysplex. With current technology the distance between a Sysplex Timer and a processor is 3 km, but it can be extended up to 26 kilometers with a special (RPQ) feature. To eliminate Timer's Single Point of Failure, it is advisable to have a Duplex Timer which is a high availability option designed to protect against hardware failure within the Timer. Also in this case the distance between the two timers is 3 Km, again extendable to 26 with a special feature (RPQ) installed. In practice then, the two timers can be installed, one in the primary site and the other in the secondary site.

- A high-speed, highly reliable communication link, which is required to pass information among systems.

- A high performance inter-system resource serialization mechanism, which is required to ensure integrity of any shared resource. Global Resource Serialization (GRS) uses XCF services to improve Sysplex availability and manageability.

Parallel Sysplex is designed to improve the availability of a single site processing complex. However, a Parallel Sysplex configuration implemented across multiple sites can be used to provide recovery within the primary site and to support disaster recovery.

One example of how this might be done is illustrated in Figure 27. There are many variations of this concept.

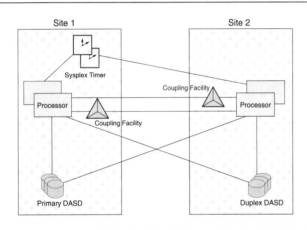

Figure 27. Combining In-house Recovery and Disaster Recovery

Two data centers are placed at a reasonable distance apart, so that there is little chance that a disaster will strike both at the same time. The distance is limited to few kilometers (less than 10) since the length of coupling links (between processors and coupling facilities) may have some impact on performance.

There are processors in both data centers, each configured as a single Parallel Sysplex. There is at least one coupling facility in each data center. (Note that access to a remote coupling facility will introduce some performance degradation, depending on the distance between the two data centers.) You may wish to have at least two coupling facilities in each data center to provide coupling facility redundancy in a disaster recovery scenario.

Two Sysplex Timers are connected together in Data Center 1 and Data Center 2 to provide redundancy. This is feasible since the distance between the two timers has been extended from few meters up to 3 Kilometers (26 Km with an optional RPQ). All processors have shared access to the primary DASD, which is located entirely in Data Center 1.

The peer-to-peer remote copy (PPRC) feature of the IBM 3990 DASD controller is used to maintain an up-to-date duplex copy of all DASD in Data Center 2. All processors can access the duplex DASD, if required.

The key advantages of this configuration are:

- The capacity at both data centers can be fully used, since workload can be dynamically scheduled across processors in both data centers using the Parallel Sysplex. None of the redundant equipment required for in-house recovery or disaster recovery needs to be idle.

- Using the Parallel Sysplex features you can recover more quickly from a single component failure in either data center.

- Recovery from a disaster can be very fast or even non-disruptive in some cases.

For any component failure, a backup component is available to take over the workload. Some of these takeovers are instantaneous, while some require an application restart. In any case, most long outages caused by lengthy data recovery processes can be avoided.

In simple terms, this is how it works:

- Recovering from a processor failure

If any processor fails, dynamic workload balancing can direct the affected workload to other processors in the Sysplex. The recovery can be nondisruptive.

- Recovering from a DASD failure

  Failure of duplex DASD in Data Center 2 can be nondisruptive, as it has no immediate effect on any active resource.

  Failure of primary DASD in Data Center 1 can be recovered by switching to the duplex copy in Data Center 2. Sometimes the address spaces that use the failed device need to be restarted to access the duplex device. P/DAS (Peer to Peer Dynamic Address Switching) is a new function that can swap allocations to the secondary device so that restarting subsystems can be avoided.

- Recovering from a disaster

  You may choose to run with all the active structures in the coupling facility at Data Center 1. The coupling facility at Data Center 2 is therefore used only for backup. In this case, after a disaster at Data Center 2, the processors at Data Center 1 can take over the workload dynamically. Primary DASD is not affected and all lock information is still available in the coupling facility in Data Center 1, so the takeover is nondisruptive.

  After a disaster at Data Center 1, the processors at Data Center 2 are available to run the workload. Because of the loss of communication with the processors and the coupling facility in Data Center 1, a full system restart is required at Data Center 2, including allocation of the duplex DASD in Data Center 2 and backout of incomplete transactions at the time of failure. This is essentially the same as if there were no Parallel Sysplex.

  The capabilities of the Parallel Sysplex towards non-disruptive workload takeover will develop further in the future. Today, what benefits most from this technology is daily operation, by interconnecting processors and sharing workloads and data. If you plan on splitting your processor resources between two sites for disaster recovery purposes, Parallel Sysplex provides an ideal vehicle to integrate the processors and spread the workload to make the split transparent.

This is just a simplified example. There are many expansions and variations to this concept. In order to work, the concept of resource duplexing needs to include not only processors and DASD, but also things such as network front-ends, consoles, tapes, and printers.

Some enterprises may deem the separation offered by Sysplex to be sufficient, as it provides protection from many forms of disaster such as fire damage and power loss.

Database Management Systems - DB2, IMS, and CICS

Perhaps the most difficult area in data recovery following a disaster is recovering the orphan data. Orphan data, as discussed in "Orphan Data" on page 53, is the data that was input into the system before the disaster occurred, but after the last data backup was taken. Unless this data can be recreated, it is lost; it may represent many hours of crucial business transactions.

When the business data is managed by a Database Management System (DBMS) such as DB2 or IMS/ESA, other options are available to minimize the amount of data that is lost. As data managed by the DBMS is updated, a continual record of all updates is kept. These records are known as log records and the data sets in which they are recorded are called the log data set. Database recovery, then, consists of restoring the latest backup of the database and then applying all the updates in the log file that have occurred since that backup was taken. If this log data can be periodically written to tape and transported off-site, the amount of orphan data can be reduced dramatically.

DB2 and IMS/ESA provide comprehensive services to produce and control backups of the database data, archive the log data, recover databases from the latest backup, and apply subsequent changes from the log. Although not actually a database, CICS/ESA provides much of this function for the VSAM data it manages. CICS/ESA maintains log records (in this case called journal records) for all updates to the VSAM data and allows the archiving of this log data periodically. A related product, CICS/VSAM Forward Recovery, can then be used to apply the log data to the latest backup of the VSAM data.

Of course, even with services available to periodically write the log data to tape, it is common for this data to remain on-site for many hours while awaiting transport off-site. The most effective way to ensure that log data is moved off-site quickly and therefore to minimize data loss is to use a product which supports electronic transfer of the log data to the alternate site. Two products that provide this service are IMS/RSR and RRDF.

IMS/ESA Remote Site Recovery (RSR)

IMS/ESA RSR is a set of features in IMS/ESA that provides a system solution for the restoration of IMS service at a remote location when the primary computing facility becomes unavailable. The functions provided by the IMS/ESA RSR features include:

- Real-time electronic log data transport to the remote site through a VTAM connection. When a log buffer is ready to be written to the log, it is sent to the remote site.

- Detection and automatic transport of missing log data. Portions of a log or entire logs could be missing at the remote site due to network problems between the primary computing facility and the remote site. RSR at the remote site will detect this situation and automatically cause RSR at the primary site to retransmit the missing log data.

- Allowance for warm starts of online systems following service restoration. The message queues containing the work awaiting processing are preserved across disaster recovery.
- The ability to maintain shadow databases. If requested, RSR maintains shadow databases at the remote site; that is, the log data that has been transported to the alternate site is continuously applied to a shadow copy of the database at that site. This eliminates the need to recover the databases when IMS service needs to be restored at the remote site. The use of this facility can reduce service outage time to a few minutes.
- Allowance for recovery of databases in parallel at the remote site. RSR at the remote site has the capability to recover multiple databases in parallel with a single pass of the log data stream.

IMS/ESA RSR offers significant advantages in the backup and recovery of IMS/ESA data. Electronic log data transport ensures that updates to IMS databases are transferred off-site almost immediately. This minimizes the loss of data in the event of a disaster. Without this capability, data loss is typically 24 hours unless you are prepared to move log data off-site manually multiple times each day.

If, in addition, you run data shadowing, not only is data loss minimized, recovery time is reduced dramatically for the shadowed data. IMS applications can be recovered and restarted in a fraction of the time otherwise required.

Because RSR is actually a part of IMS/ESA, it is well integrated with the IMS functions that manage logging, DBRC, and recovery. On the other hand, IMS/ESA RSR does not support any other Database Management Systems.

RRDF

Remote Recovery Data Facility (RRDF) is a product that
transports log/journal data and pertinent recovery control over a
VTAM connection to an alternate site. RRDF supports IMS,
CICS, and DB2. As discussed above, the main benefit of this is
the reduction of the amount of orphan data that results from a
disaster.

The primary features of RRDF are:

- Automated transmission of recovery data (logs and journals).
  As with IMS/ESA RSR, this transmission is done near-real-time
  and at the log record level.

- Detection and automatic transport of missing log data.

- DBRC synchronization. DBRC data is also transmitted to the
  alternate site to ensure synchronization.

- Avoidance of lost data due to media errors.

- Avoidance of lost data due to lost volumes.

- Optional DB2 utility to perform forward recovery (Log Apply).
  For DB2, RRDF offers the Log Apply facility, which
  continuously applies the transmitted log records to a shadow
  copy of the DB2 database located at the alternate site.

An exit in the logging routines of the DBMS is used to pass the
log data to RRDF. RRDF uses a VTAM connection to transmit
the data. For recovery, it is assumed that an image copy of the
databases will be available at the remote site, either stored there
regularly or transported to the remote site following disaster
declaration.

IMS/ESA RSR and RRDF both offer significant advantages in the
backup and recovery of database data, namely:

- Increasing the completeness of recovery by reducing the
  amount of orphan data.

- Automating the delivery of recovery data to the remote site.

- Reducing the time taken for data to be transported to the recovery site.

- When data set level tracking (DLT) is used for IMS RSR or DB2 Log Apply with RRDF it significantly reduces the time taken to recover.

One additional advantage of RRDF is that it supports multiple database types. Note, however, that RRDF does not eliminate the need to synchronize the end of log tapes from different DBMSs in recovery.

Data Facilities Storage Management System/MVS (DFSMS/MVS)

In "Data Backup and Recovery Processes" on page 46, we discuss some of the intricacies involved in the successful backup and recovery of data: ensuring that the data is consistent with other related data, backing up the data in a way that is compatible with the recovery tools and the recovery device types, and managing the data so that what is restored is complete and synchronized. DFSMS/MVS is a comprehensive product that provides a range of tools to support backup and recovery for DR.

DFSMS/MVS is the storage management subsystem for MVS. Many of the backup and recovery facilities it provides are not provided by DFSMS alone; they depend on the interaction of other hardware and software products.

This section covers the most important DFSMS functions from a disaster recovery standpoint. DFSMS/MVS is a single product comprised of a number of components:

- DFSMS/MVS Data Facilities (DFSMSdfp*)

- DFSMS/MVS Data Set Services (DFSMSdss*)

- DFSMS/MVS Hierarchical Storage Manager (DFSMShsm*)

• DFSMS/MVS Removable Media Manager (DFSMSrmm*)

Aggregate Backup and Recovery Support (ABARS)

"Interrelationships Within the Data" on page 57 points out the need to ensure that separate pieces of related data are backed up in a consistent way, usually at the same time and using a single tool. ABARS facilitates the backup of all the data related to an application and aids in packaging the data as a single entity in preparation for taking it off-site. This enables the recovery of individual applications in user-priority sequence.

ABARS is a function of DFSMShsm, a component of DFSMS/MVS. ABARS writes groups of data sets (aggregates) and control information as tape files. ABARS enables remote recovery of critical business applications, transfer of workloads, and distribution of data. ABARS allows up to 15 copies of the aggregate to be made.

User-defined recovery procedures can be backed up to an optional instruction/activity log file.

The aggregate control file contains control information to assist in the recovery of the data. For instance, ABARS uses the data set information in this file to allocate empty data sets that are required to recover an application and to catalog large tape data sets that are not on the aggregate data file.

ABARS gives you the ability to backup and recover applications as separate entities. Where data sets are unique to an application, this application can be recovered independently at the alternate site, resulting in far more recovery flexibility. The more critical workloads can be recovered first and processing can begin while other applications are still being recovered. Data management is also improved in this situation, since all the data required to recover a given application exists in a single identifiable set of tapes. Where data sets are shared between applications you can do the following: these applications can be combined into one aggregate, the shared data sets can be backed up as part of only one of the aggregates, or a separate "shared" aggregate can be created.

Concurrent Copy

As data processing moves increasingly towards continuous availability services, organizations are facing the dilemma of finding an appropriate time at which to stop access to the data to allow a consistent backup. In the case of database data, services have been available for some time to enable a copy of the database even while updates to that data continue. In many cases these services are adequate; however, they do have two limitations. First, the database copy can not be synchronized easily with other backups, and second, they only apply to database data.

Concurrent Copy provides a consistent, point-in-time copy across multiple data sets or databases even while updates to this data continue.

Concurrent Copy is a facility provided by DFSMS/MVS and the 3990 Model 003 and Model 006 DASD Controllers. It allows a point-in-time copy of data to be made even while the data is available for update. Updating of the data must be stopped only while the copy is being requested (typically measured in seconds). Once the request has been accepted, updates may be resumed and Concurrent Copy will create a copy of the data as it was when the copy request was issued. This facility dramatically reduces the time a database or data set must be unavailable to take a backup copy.

DFSMSdss provides access to the Concurrent Copy facility. Most of the Concurrent Copy work is not executed by DFSMSdss but by the System Data Mover(SDM), a function within DFSMS/MVS. When a copy request is received through DFSMSdss, SDM initializes the environment ready for the copy.

This includes informing the 3990 of the data extents to be copied.

Once the environment is initialized, the copy is started and updates to the data can resume. The main steps in this operation are shown in Figure 28. If any updates are received for data sets being copied (1), and if the portion of data to be updated has not already been copied, this data is copied to a sidefile in the 3990 cache (2), and the update is allowed to complete. To minimize the requirement for cache storage, data is moved from the cache sidefiles to a dataspace sidefile in MVS (3). In copying the data, DFSMSdss always searches the sidefiles before the disk; hence, the backup (4) does not include any of the updates made since the copy request was accepted.

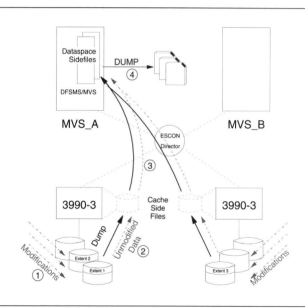

Figure 28. Concurrent Copy

Data Facility Removable Media Manager (DFSMSrmm)

Although a range of options for the electronic transfer of recovery data now exists, (see "Loss of Transactions" on page 30), there is still widespread use of magnetic tape cartridge for the backup and transport of disaster recovery data. The use of tapes is straightforward and most importantly, it is relatively inexpensive. However, if recovery from a disaster is to be efficient and successful, tape use and transport must be very well-managed. In a disaster, *all* of the tapes at the primary site may be gone. It is no good to find out at this point that the procedures for tape management were inadequate and that certain critical data is now missing.

DFSMSrmm is the component of DFSMS/MVS that manages removable media. DFSMSrmm deals with both *data sets* and *volumes*. These may be managed across multiple locations and may reside inside or outside an automated tape library.

In an enterprise, there are normally one or more tape libraries that must be managed. DFSMSrmm allows all tapes to be managed as one enterprise-wide library, even across sites. It keeps track of tapes located in system-managed libraries and DFSMSrmm shelf space.

A system-managed tape library can either be an automated tape library or a manual tape library, consisting of tape units, tapes, and tape storage.

Storage locations are physically distinct locations where volumes are stored when they are removed from the media library for disaster recovery purposes or vital records retention. DFSMSrmm can support up to three storage locations. These are:

- Local
- Distant
- Remote

A tape can be moved between the storage locations and the system-managed libraries, and this movement is tracked by DFSMSrmm.

In planning for disaster recovery, effective tape management is vital. Recovery can be delayed if the required data is not easily accessible at the recovery site at the right time. The delay may be even more significant if the required data is missing. Whether you are continuously transporting tapes to the alternate site or only moving them to the alternate site in the event of a disaster, DFSMSrmm offers the functions to efficiently manage and locate backup data as required.

ADSTAR Distributed Storage Manager (ADSM)

"Data Backup and Recovery Processes" on page 46 discusses the many considerations to address when backing up a large collection of varied but interrelated data. However, if these backups are carefully planned and maintained, disaster recovery can be made successful. When all data is managed centrally, the regular backup of the data can be reasonably straightforward. When the data is distributed between many sites and across multiple processing platforms, this task can become far more complex.

As data is distributed more widely, the responsibility for the correct backup and retrieval of that data often falls to the individual user. In some cases these users are ill-equipped for this responsibility.

ADSM is a distributed client/server program that provides storage management and data access capabilities for clients in a heterogeneous network environment.

The Storage Management Services of ADSM provide an automated, high performance network-based backup and archive product for workstations and LAN file servers. They consist of an MVS, or VM-based backup and archive server and backup and archive clients, including OS/2, AIX for RISC System/6000, DOS, SunOS, Solaris, Apple Macintosh Operating System, Microsoft Windows, HP-UX, DEC ULTRIX, SCO UNIX 386, OS/2 DBCS, Novell NetWare 386, AT&T UNIX SVR4 MP-RAS, Siemens Nixdorf SINIX-Z, DOS DBCS, Windows DBCS, Siemens Nixdorf SINIX RISC, Microsoft Windows NT, NEC EWS-UX/V, Silicon Graphics IRIX, and Sequent PTX. ADSM is one of a multi-platform family of products. Other products in this family run on VSE/ESA, OS/400, AIX/600, OS/2, SUN Solaris, and HP-UX.

ADSM extends the DFSMS philosophy of storage management to the distributed environment, allowing users to establish policies to manage data availability, data recoverability, and storage resources on heterogeneous platforms or networks. It builds on the concepts of DFSMS, allowing you to establish consistent storage management policies across your enterprise.

ADSM Storage Management Services provides automated, centrally scheduled, unattended backups for clients. ADSM backup and archive data is especially suited for utilizing the System/390 strengths of managing large amounts of data on direct-access storage devices (DASD) or Tape. Once a workstation is registered, it is provided with the following services:

- A centrally scheduled policy-managed backup/archive facility

  Users can specify how frequently to backup a file, the maximum number of backup versions of a file to retain, and how long to retain these backup versions.

- System-assisted restore of backed-up files

  Users can restore single or multiple files, directories, or complete file systems.

- User-initiated archival and retrieval of file-server and workstation clients files

  Archive allows users to store their low-use files, allowing them to free up space on their local disk for other uses.

Users can obtain information on their backed-up and archived files from the ADSM database. They can specify a variety of selection criteria (such as name filters or archive dates) as part of their information request. This information can then be used when restoring a file.

Appendix B. Disaster Recovery Tiers - SHARE 78 Definition

There are many different ways to describe or categorize different disaster recovery solutions. In "Design the Backup/Recovery Solution" on page 43, some of the main characteristics of these solutions are discussed, including:

- Scope of backup/recovery
- Status of disaster recovery plan
- Distance between the sites
- How the sites are interconnected
- How the data is transported between sites
- How much data is lost
- How up-to-date the data at the alternate site is maintained
- How ready the alternate site is to begin recovery

At SHARE 78, Anaheim, 1992, in session M028, the Automated Remote Site Recovery Task Force presented seven tiers of recoverability:

Tier 0   No off-site Data

Provides no preparation either in saving information, determining requirements, establishing a backup hardware platform, or developing a contingency plan.

Tier 1   *Pickup Truck* Access Method (PTAM)

To be at tier one, an installation would need to develop a contingency plan, back up required information and store it in contingency storage (off-site location), determine recovery requirements, and optionally establish a backup platform supporting a conditioned facility, without processing hardware.

Tier 2   PTAM + Hot Site

Encompasses all requirements of tier one and would require a backup platform to have sufficient hardware and network resources to support the installation's critical processing requirements. Processing is considered critical if it must be supported on hardware existing at the time of the disaster.

Tier 3   Electronic Vaulting

Encompasses all the requirements of tier two and, in addition, supports electronic vaulting of some subset of the information. The receiving hardware must be physically separated from the primary platform and the data stored for recovery after the disaster.

Tier 4   Active Secondary Site

Introduces the requirements of (1) active management of the recovery data by a CPU at the recovery site and (2) bi-directional recovery. The receiving hardware must be physically separated from the primary platform.

Tier 5   Two-Site Two-Phase Commit

Encompasses all the requirements of tier four and, in addition, will maintain selected data in image status (updates will be applied to both the local and remote copies of the data bases within a single commit scope). Tier five requires both the primary and secondary platforms' data to be updated before the update request is considered satisfied. Tier five requires partially or fully dedicated hardware on the secondary platform with the capability to automatically transfer the workload to the secondary platform.

Tier 6   Zero Data Loss

Encompasses zero loss of data and immediate and automatic transfer to the secondary platform. Data is considered lost if "ENTER" has been accepted (at the terminal) but the request has not been satisfied.

Note: SHARE is an organization made up of data processing users.

These tiers may be useful in a general measurement or ranking of disaster recovery solutions; however, their ability to describe or categorize specific solutions is limited. Due to the many possible permutations of the different variables in a solution, it is impossible to properly describe all potential solutions with a small number of tiers. For example, a bi-directional recovery that uses manual tape transport only can be considered a Tier 1 as well as a Tier 4 solution.

This problem is exacerbated by the introduction of new products. For instance, 3990-6 Peer-to-Peer Remote Copy provides a synchronous data copy as described in Tier 5. However it has no active processor managing this data, which would imply it is lower than Tier 4. (PPRC was not announced when SHARE defined the tiers and therefore was not catered for.)

The aim of this discussion is not to criticize the tiers defined by SHARE. The definitions are sensible and useful as far as they go. The point is that solution design in the area of disaster recovery is a highly complex activity and the use of generic categories can sometimes lead to an over-simplification in our description. We feel it is better to define a specific solution more fully by describing all of its characteristics. This leads to a better communication of what is being planned, and avoids the danger of ambiguity in the design.

Appendix C. Special Notices

This publication is intended to assist the customer in designing, implementing, and operating a disaster recovery site. The information in this publication is not intended as the specification of any programming interfaces that are provided by the products mentioned. See the PUBLICATIONS section of the IBM Programming Announcement for these products for more information about what publications are considered to be product documentation.

References in this publication to IBM products, programs or services do not imply that IBM intends to make these available in all countries in which IBM operates. Any reference to an IBM product, program, or service is not intended to state or imply that only IBM's product, program, or service may be used. Any functionally equivalent program that does not infringe any of IBM's intellectual property rights may be used instead of the IBM product, program or service.

Information in this book was developed in conjunction with use of the equipment specified, and is limited in application to those specific hardware and software products and levels.

IBM may have patents or pending patent applications covering subject matter in this document. The furnishing of this document does not give you any license to these patents. You can send license inquiries, in writing, to the IBM Director of Licensing, IBM Corporation, 500 Columbus Avenue, Thornwood, NY 10594 USA.

Licensees of this program who wish to have information about it for the purpose of enabling: (i) the exchange of information between independently created programs and other programs (including this one) and (ii) the mutual use of the information which has been exchanged, should contact IBM Corporation, Dept. 600A, Mail Drop 1329, Somers, NY 10589 USA.

Such information may be available, subject to appropriate terms and conditions, including in some cases, payment of a fee.

The information contained in this document has not been submitted to any formal IBM test and is distributed AS IS. The information about non-IBM ("vendor") products in this manual has been supplied by the vendor and IBM assumes no responsibility for its accuracy or completeness. The use of this information or the implementation of any of these techniques is a customer responsibility and depends on the customer's ability to evaluate and integrate them into the customer's operational environment. While each item may have been reviewed by IBM for accuracy in a specific situation, there is no guarantee that the same or similar results will be obtained elsewhere. Customers attempting to adapt these techniques to their own environments do so at their own risk.

The following document contains examples of data and reports used in daily business operations. To illustrate them as completely as possible, the examples contain the names of individuals, companies, brands, and products. All of these names are fictitious and any similarity to the names and addresses used by an actual business enterprise is entirely coincidental.

The following terms are trademarks of the International Business Machines Corporation in the United States and/or other countries:

ADSTAR	AIX
AS/400	CICS
CICS/ESA	DB2
DFSMS	DFSMS/MVS
DFSMSdfp	DFSMSdss
DFSMShsm	DFSMSrmm

Enterprise System/9000	ES/9000
ESA/390	ESCON
ESCON XDF	IBM
IMS	IMS/ESA
Integrated Systems Solutions	ISSC
MVS/DFP	MVS/ESA
NetView	OS/2
OS/400	Parallel Sysplex
PR/SM	PROFS
RISC System/6000	RRDF
S/370	S/390
SAA	Sysplex Timer
System/38	System/390
SystemView	VM/XA
VSE/ESA	VTAM
VTAM	VTAM
3090	

The following terms are trademarks of other companies:

C-bus is a trademark of Corollary, Inc.

PC Direct is a trademark of Ziff Communications Company and is used by IBM Corporation under license.

UNIX is a registered trademark in the United States and other countries licensed exclusively through X/Open Company Limited.

Microsoft, Windows, and the Windows 95 logo are trademarks or registered trademarks of Microsoft Corporation.

Java and HotJava are trademarks of Sun Microsystems, Inc.

Other trademarks are trademarks of their respective companies.

Appendix D. Related Publications

The publications listed in this section are considered particularly suitable for a more detailed discussion of the topics covered in this book.

International Technical Support Organization Publications

For information on ordering these ITSO publications see "How To Get ITSO Redbooks" on page 195.

- *Disaster Recovery Library S/390 Technology Guide*, GG24-4210
- *Disaster Recovery Library Data Recovery*, GG24-3994

A complete list of International Technical Support Organization publications, known as redbooks, with a brief description of each, may be found in:

International Technical Support Organization Bibliography of Redbooks, GG24-3070.

How To Get ITSO Redbooks

This section explains how you can find out about ITSO redbooks, CD-ROMs, workshops, and residencies. A form for ordering books and CD-ROMs is also provided.

This information was current at the time of publication, but is continually subject to change. The latest information may be found at URL http://www.redbooks.ibm.com.

- **Online Orders** (Do not send credit card information over the Internet) — send orders to:

	IBMMAIL	Internet
In United States:	usib6fpl at ibmmail	usib6fpl@ibmmail.com
In Canada:	caibmbkz at ibmmail	lmannix@vnet.ibm.com
Other Countries:	bookshop at dkibmbsh at ibmmail	bookshop@dk.ibm.com

- **Telephone orders**

United States (toll free)	1-800-879-2755
Canada (toll free)	1-800-IBM-4YOU

Outside North America	(long distance charges apply)
(+45) 4810-1320 - Danish	(+45) 4810-1020 - German
(+45) 4810-1420 - Dutch	(+45) 4810-1620 - Italian
(+45) 4810-1540 - English	(+45) 4810-1270 - Norwegian
(+45) 4810-1670 - Finnish	(+45) 4810-1120 - Spanish
(+45) 4810-1220 - French	(+45) 4810-1170 - Swedish

- **Mail Orders** — send orders to:

IBM Publications	IBM Publications	IBM Direct Services
Customer Support	144-4th Avenue, S.W.	Sortemosevej 21
P.O. Box 29554	Calgary, Alberta T2P 3N5	DK-3450 Allerød
Raleigh, NC 27626-0570	Canada	Denmark
USA		

- **Fax** — send orders to:

United States (toll free)	1-800-445-9269	
Canada (toll free)	1-800-267-4455	
Outside North America	(+45) 48 14 2207	(long distance charge)

- **1-800-IBM-4FAX (United States)** or **(+1) 415 855 43 29 (Outside USA)** —
  ask for:

  Index # 4421 Abstracts of new redbooks
  Index # 4422 IBM redbooks
  Index # 4420 Redbooks for last six months

- **Direct Services** - send note to softwareshop@vnet.ibm.com

- **On the World Wide Web**

  Redbooks Home Page   http://www.redbooks.ibm.com
  IBM Direct Publications Catalog   http://www.elink.ibmlink.ibm.com/pbl/pbl

- **Internet Listserver**

  With an Internet E-mail address, anyone can subscribe to an IBM
  Announcement Listserver. To initiate the service, send an E-mail note to
  announce@webster.ibmlink.ibm.com with the keyword subscribe in the body
  of the note (leave the subject line blank).

IBM Redbook Order Form

Please send me the following:

Title	Order Number	Quantity

☐ **Please put me on the mailing list for updated versions of the IBM Redbook Catalog**

First Name	Last Name	
Company		
Address		
City	Postal Code	Country
Telephone Number	Telefax Number	VAT

☐ Invoice to Customer Number _____

☐ Credit Card Number _____

Credit Card Expiration Date	Card Issued to	Signature

We accept American Express, Diners, Eurocard, Master Card, and Visa. Payment by credit card not available in all countries. Signature mandatory for Credit Card Payment.

DO NOT SEND CREDIT CARD INFORMATION OVER THE INTERNET.

Glossary

This glossary includes the definition of terms as they are used in this book. Note that in other contexts these terms may be defined differently.

Alternate site. Another site or facility, such as a commercial hot site or a customer-owned second site, that will become the recovery site in the event of a disaster.

Application. A collection of related DP jobs or online systems designed to support the business processes.

Availability. A measure of how much (often specified as a percentage) the data processing services are available to the users in a specified time frame.

Backup. A spare resource that can be used in place of a failed resource.

Back up. To copy a resource or data to enable recovery in the event of a loss of that resource or data.

Business Process. A group of related activities that support the successful operation of the business or its services.

Catch-up data. Data and data updates generated by the business during the outage, which have to be subsequently entered into the recovered system.

Cold site. A recovery site that may be equipped with a DP infrastructure (for example, a raised floor, air conditioning, or even network connections), but with little or no DP equipment installed.

Commit. In data processing the point at which the data updates are written to the database in a way which is irrevocable.

Continuous availability. The elimination or masking of both planned and unplanned outages, so that no system outages are apparent to the end user. Continuous availability can also be stated as the ability to operate 24 hours/day, 7 days/week, with no outages apparent to the end user.

Continuous operations. The elimination or masking of planned outages. A system that delivers continuous operations is a system that has no scheduled outages.

Criticality Level. Relative rank on a scale which indicates the priority or importance of a business process, an application or of data. Criticality level may also be used synonymously with the maximum acceptable outage for a business process or application.

Data currency. A measure of how close the restored data level matches the data level at the time of the disaster. Usually data can be restored to the level of the most recent backup or to that of accumulated transaction logs. This level may be different from the level that existed at the time of the disaster.

Database Management System (DBMS). A supervisory system which controls and manages the database data associated with it.

Data Processing (DP). All that has to do with computers and their supporting environment, such as hardware, software, data, networks, operators, programmers, and so on. It is a more global or modern version of DP.

Disaster. An event that renders DP services unavailable for a period so long that the DP facilities must be moved to another site.

Forward Recovery. Reconstructing a file or database by applying changes to an older version (backup or image copy) with data recorded in a log data set. The sequence of changes to the restored copy is in the same order in which they were originally made.

Gigabytes. A measurement of processor or disk storage (one billion bytes).

Hot site. A recovery site with all the required IT equipment installed. In many cases, this term is used to mean specifically a hot site service offered by a third party.

Image Copy. A backup copy of a data base, typically on portable storage media (for example, tape). Image copies are usually created through backup functions built into the database system and contain all information and metadata required to restore the data base to a consistent and usable state.

Infrastructure. In conjunction with DP, the term often refers to peripheral facilities required by medium or large computer environments. It includes, for instance, air conditioning, water cooling, electrical power, access to communications networks, and raised floors.

Megabytes. A measurement of processor or disk storage (one million bytes).

Orphan data. Data that has been entered at the primary data center but had not been transferred to the alternate data center at the time of the disaster. This data has to be re-entered to provide data integrity.

Outage. Any period of time (within defined service hours) when the data processing service is not available to the user.

Periodic Backup. A data recovery methodology where the installation will quiesce the application, back up everything required to recover **to that point,** and send the data to another location.

Ready-to-Roll-Forward. A data recovery methodology where the installation performs periodic backups, but also sends complete data update logs to another location. Transport may be by physical or electronic media. Recovery will be to the last log file received at the recovery site.

Realtime-Remote-Update. The capability to update the primary and recovery copies of data prior to sending the transaction response or completing a program or task.

Realtime-Roll-Forward. A data recovery methodology similar to roll-forward, except that updates are transmitted and applied at the same time they are being logged in the production site. This *near real time* transmission and application of log data would not impact transaction response time at the production site.

Recovery. The process of using alternate resources to restore data processing to an operable state after a failure.

Remote Operations. The ability to perform operations tasks from a remote location.

Remote Site Recovery. The ability to continue or resume processing of the critical workload

at a remote site in the event of a primary outage.

Roll-Forward. A data recovery methodology where a *shadow* copy of the data is maintained on disk at the recovery site. As complete log files are received, they are applied to the *shadow* copy using recovery utilities. Transmission may be physical or electronic media. This term is often used interchangeably with the term *Forward Recovery*.

Scope of Failure. The magnitude of a failure (for instance, the number of components failing at one time) and the anticipated repair time.

Second site. Refers to a company-owned second site that can be used as a recovery facility if the company's primary site is destroyed.

Service level agreement. Contract between DP, business units, and users which describes the scope of services, performance, and infrastructure that are delivered by DP and used by the business units and users.

Single point of failure. An essential resource for which there is no backup.

List of Abbreviations

ABARS   aggregate backup and recovery support (feature of DFHSM 2.5)

ADSM   ADSTAR Distributed Storage Manager

AIX   advanced interactive executive (IBM's flavor of UNIX)

APA   all points addressable

AT&T   American Telephone & Telegraph Company

CEO   chief executive officer

CICS   customer information control system (IBM)

CMOS   complementary metal oxide semiconductor

CPU   central processing unit

CTC   channel to channel

DASD   direct access storage device

DBMS   data base management system (System/38)

DBRC   data base recovery control (IMS)

DEC   Digital Equipment Corporation (USA)

DFM   Distributed File Manager (part of DFSMS/MVS, see: DFM/MVS)

DFSMS/MVS   Data Facility Storage Management Subsystem/MVS

DOS   disk operating system (PC and 370 system)

DP   data processing

DR   disaster recovery

DRC   disaster recovery coordinator

DRP   disaster recovery plan

IBM   International Business Machines Corporation

ESCON   enterprise systems connection (architecture, IBM System/390)

I/O   input/output

IMS/ESA   information management system/enterprise systems architecture

ISSC   IBM Division 07 (ISSC), Integrated Systems Solutions Corporation

IT   information technology

ITSO	International Technical Support Organization	**RRDF**	remote recovery data facility (IMS/ESA)
LAN	local area network	**SHARE**	an association of IBM engineering/scientific customers with large computing systems
LED	light emitting diode		
LPAR	logically partitioned mode		
MIPS	million instructions per second	**SNA**	systems network architecture (IBM)
MVS	multiple virtual storage (IBM System 370 and 390)	**SPE**	small programming enhancement
		UNIX	an operating system developed at Bell Laboratories (trademark of UNIX System Laboratories, licensed exclusively by X/Open Company, Ltd.)
MVS/DFP	multiple virtual storage/data facility product (IBM)		
MVS/ESA	multiple virtual storage/enterprise systems architecture (IBM)		
NCP	network control program	**UPS**	uninterruptible power supply/system
OCR	optical character recognition	**VSAM**	virtual storage access method (IBM)
PPRC	Peer-to-Peer Remote Copy (IBM 3990 Model 6)	**VTAM**	virtual telecommunications access method (IBM) (runs under MVS, VM, and DOS/VSE)
PROFS	Professional Office System		
PTF	program temporary fix		
RISC	reduced instruction set computer/cycles	**XDF**	extended distance feature (ESCON)
RMM	Removable Media Manager (IBM program product)	**XRC**	Extended Remote Copy (IBM 3990 Model 6)

Index

R

Prentice Hall PTR Online!

LOCATION: http://www.prenhall.com/divisions/ptr/

plug into
Prentice Hall PTR Online!

Thank you for purchasing this Prentice Hall PTR book. As a professional, we know that having information about the latest technology at your fingertips is essential. Keep up-to-date about Prentice Hall PTR on the World Wide Web.

Visit the Prentice Hall PTR Web page at
http://www.prenhall.com/divisions/ptr/
and get the latest information about:

➢ **New Books, Software & Features of the Month**

➢ **New Book and Series Home Pages**

➢ **Stores that Sell Our Books**

➢ **Author Events and Trade Shows**

 join prentice hall ptr's new internet mailing lists!

Each month, subscribers to our mailing lists receive two e-mail messages highlighting recent releases, author events, new content on the Prentice Hall PTR web site, and where to meet us at professional meetings. Join one, a few, *or all* of our mailing lists in targeted subject areas in Computers and Engineering.

Visit the Mailroom at http://www.prenhall.com/mail_lists/
to subscribe to our mailing lists in...

COMPUTER SCIENCE:

Programming and Methodologies
Communications
Operating Systems
Database Technologies

ENGINEERING:

Electrical Engineering
Chemical and Environmental Engineering
Mechanical and Civil Engineering
Industrial Engineering and Quality

 PTR / PH

get connected with prentice hall ptr online!